MW00465344

"Satish Rao's glass is always half-full rather than half-empty. Through this book, he conveys his life and appreciation for the values of hard work, honesty, and integrity. During the years we worked together, I gained a deep appreciation for his motivation to live up to his fullest potential in the industry. This book is a rich and rewarding read."

Dr. James Albrecht
(Retd.) Group Vice-President- Asia/Pacific,
McCormick & Co. Inc. USA

"Satish Rao transmits his cheerfulness, friendliness, and optimism through this book. He has translated how he always found a way to take everything in life as a learning opportunity to grow through this book."

Lata Pillai
Managing Director & Head – Capital Markets
JLL India

"Among the array of motivational books talking about the aggressive approach to accomplishing ambition, here comes an author who empirically endorses the importance of values, ethics, and humility. Simplistic yet highly sophisticated virtues may be hard to implement but immensely rewarding in deeper satisfaction and creating a culture to benefit generations. I would strongly recommend it to my millennial son."

Dr. Rajesh Shah, MD
Medical thinker, researcher,
homeopath, and author

"Satish Rao, Chairman and Managing Director at Firmenich India Aromatics Ltd, now does the unbelievable: A very well scripted, finely curated, thought-provoking, slice of life book embellished with real-life experiences. This a must-read for teenagers, adolescents, young & not so young who are getting ready to take a flight in their careers."

Mary Joseph
Retd. Principal
Lokmanya Tilak High School

"After reading the chapter Chawl to CEO, I find that Satish Rao has succinctly translated his life's experiences into words, something all writers strive for but succeed only so often. He stays focused on his vision while being honest in his stories. I am sure that this book, with its anecdotal events and easy reading style, will help everyone accomplish their dreams."

Roopam Kapoor
Chief Commissioner of Customs, Mumbai

"Satish Rao is a wonderful example of humility, commitment and competence. He rose through the ranks, has lived all over the world and currently leads Firmenich in India. In his book, Satish talks about dreaming big, following one's passion, being humble and being grounded in a firm value system. He is an alumnus of Somaiya Vidyavihar and we are proud to have him as a wonderful role model for our students to follow."

Samir Somaiya
Chancellor, Somaiya Vidyavihar University

CAN I FLY?
GIVING WINGS TO YOUR DREAMS

SATISH RAO

STARDOM BOOKS

STARDOM BOOKS

WORLDWIDE

www.StardomBooks.com

STARDOM BOOKS

A Division of Stardom Publishing

and infoYOGIS Technologies.

105-501 Silverside Road

Wilmington, DE 19809

FIRST EDITION DECEMBER 2021

Stardom Books

CAN I FLY?
GIVING WINGS TO YOUR DREAMS

SATISH RAO

p. 168
cm. 13.5 X 21.5

Category: SELF-HELP/MOTIVATIONAL &
INSPIRATIONAL

ISBN-13: 978-1-7369486-7-5

DEDICATION

To my late aunt and uncle, Mrs. Vimala Rao and Mr. Vittal Rao, who raised me at their home as parents. Through this amazing couple, I learned the values of humility, integrity, and nurturing relationships.

CONTENTS

ACKNOWLEDGMENTS

I want to take this opportunity to thank my wife, Jyothi, and daughter Nidhi for motivating me to write this book. As much as they were inspirational, they were also the best critics of my book, ensuring that I capture the life incidents objectively and helping to derive lessons from them. I would also like to extend my gratitude to all my dear friends who pushed me to embark on this journey.

PREFACE

I have never written a book in my life. You may then wonder why this attempt? I still do not know if I am capable enough to distill my thoughts immaculately into a book. However, I was inspired to write this book after reading many books on how to be successful. They are excellent reads and do provide you with enough information on how you can be successful in a business and corporate environment. However, I noted that while they spoke of the skills needed and how to hone them, they rarely spelled out the soft virtues required to climb up the corporate ladder and remain successful at high leadership positions. These traits are immensely needed to supplement the hard skills of leadership. Hence, with this book, I make my humble attempt to focus on those critical soft virtues required in life to be successful and happy. I have cited many examples from real life and my own experiences, which shaped my life learnings. I hope, dear reader, that these incidences of success and failure give you a good perspective on articulating your own life formula to accomplish your dreams.

PART A: GENESIS OF A DREAM

1

CHAWL TO CEO

"If you have built castles in the air, your work need not be lost; that is where they should be. Now put the foundations under them."
— Henry David Thoreau

I wanted to be a CEO by the age of 45.

I was not born with this desire. However, it became the driving force of my life once I graduated from college. For the reader to understand how that came to be, I would have to start at the beginning. I was born in Mumbai, the city of dreams. My early childhood memories are filled with fun. Unlike today, we did not own a television set or have access to the Internet back then.

Our only source of entertainment was playing on the streets; all the neighborhood children played together. Our streets not only served as our playground, but also, many a time, provided us with the equipment to play with. All we had to bring out with us was a cricket ball. We would collect some stones and stack them up in a pile. We divided ourselves into various teams; one team would nominate a hitter whose aim would be to knock off the stack. I am sure by now, most of you might have recognized the game. You are right. It is *Lagori*.

I never realized it then, but the neighbors and my family were a community. Living in Mumbai, our streets doubled as playgrounds, and they were flanked by yellow greying buildings. These buildings were at most three stories tall. Their walls probably had not seen a fresh coat of paint ever since they were built. Each of these buildings had around six families living on each floor. Every floor had its own balcony and front yard. The building's shared walking space usually doubled up as a balcony and front yard for every house. We did not mind the communal nature of our residences.

As children, we came to think of these shared spaces in front of our homes as our personal stands from which our families viewed our games. A typical day began with our parents waking us all up. Those who had to attend school would start getting ready. The others got some time to lie around on their beds for a little longer while our parents got ready.

However, if we wanted to have our breakfast, we had to get up before 7:30 am. I usually had *mandakki* for breakfast; this is a famous dish from Karnataka. Most of you might know it as *Poha* or flattened rice. It is a savory dish with the right kick of spice to get you ready for the long day. Our fathers used to take us to our schools before they left for their factories. Our classmates and peers at school generally were all from the same neighborhood or colonies. A colony basically comprised of a group of adjacent buildings that formed a society of like-minded people. All of us got together and celebrated festivals as one large family: Ganesh Chaturthi, Janmashtami, and Diwali, to name some.

Each of our colonies would collect money to install a temporary shrine for Lord Ganesha during the months of August and September. One person was appointed in each colony to take care of the funds and organize all the activities. In my society, the person in charge was Mr. Yadav. He was a man with a serious face. Even though he was not the tallest person in the colony during my childhood, his bearing and stature made him seem bigger than the rest. He organized some of the most memorable occasions within our society.

He was one of the very few people who held a management position in the society, which was otherwise populated mostly by factory workers. I was never aware of the differences between the living conditions of my family and that of those who hailed from a better background. My world revolved around the dusty streets where I played with my friends and family. Our building may not have been palatial, but it was our home. We enjoyed bonhomie and camaraderie. Every year we used to have a sports event; the entire society would celebrate it together. I especially remember the musical chair competition, which used to have the latest Bollywood hits booming out of the speakers. However, when I was six, I happened to visit South Mumbai, and this is when it hit me that I was just a frog in the pond all along. South Mumbai was like a whole other world.

How did I happen to visit South Mumbai when I was six? Well, some of our parents had banded together to form a group party to chaperone my friends and me to the beach. They chose South Mumbai, which featured spots like Juhu, Worli, etc. I still remember that trip, traveling via train and then by bus. The scale of the buildings stunned me. The edifices of these buildings seemingly towered into the sky in a beguiling mix of glass panels and bright colors. However, it was the beach that truly bowled me over. I saw the turquoise water gleam, but my eyes were taken in by the shine of the beach houses.

I remember remarking to my mother by pointing to one beach house, "Amma! I finally see one building which is the same size as ours. But why are not there many children in that apartment?" My mother smiled and said, "Son, that is one house. Only one family lives there." I was stunned. It took me a while to reconcile to the fact that houses could be of such scale. I immediately shared this nugget of information with my friends. Those who had come to this area for the first time like me were equally flabbergasted. However, those who had already made this trip before were not as responsive. For the first time in my life, 'rich' went from just a word to a practical chasm.

Before my trip to South Mumbai, I thought my family was rich, and my schoolmates were rich. I had no reason to doubt it. We had a roof over our heads. We ate three meals a day. We all could go to school. We had some of the most enjoyable festival celebrations. With time, I realized that we were rich in every measure except in material terms. But at that moment, a six-year-old boy became aware for the first time that the world outside was incredibly more complex than the world he lived in. He wanted to cross that gap.

I wanted to be a CEO by the age of 45.

An equally vivid day from my childhood was during my sixth grade. I can recall it as if it was yesterday. It was swelteringly hot, and the monsoon was late. The month of June generally marked a period of fun. It was the beginning of the school year. My school was located at a slightly lower level compared to the area around it. So, whenever it rained, the water from the surrounding areas would drain into the school.

This meant that there were days when we students had to help in draining out the flood water from our school premises. We each used a bucket or a mug to scoop the water and throw it outside. For children who loved to dance and prance around in joy in the rain, these activities meant a lot of fun. However, our seniors and teachers always looked at us with red eyes whenever they caught us having fun in such situations. They used to reprimand us for playing around. I never understood their anger. How could they not have fun?

Anyway, our school might not have been the best, infrastructure-wise. But it surely was the best, faculty-wise. One of my favorite teachers was Shetty Teacher. Of course, I can now say that with hindsight. However, as students, we greatly feared her. She was a disciplinarian.

Even the noisiest class would turn silent once her shadow made its presence known. When it was time for her class, even the troublemakers would quiet down and not let out a squeak as the bell went marking the end of the previous class.

She would walk into the classroom and read out the names from the attendance register. If you came in late, you had to go to the back of the class and stand for the rest of the period. She seemed frail, but her presence was magnetic. Perhaps it was because she taught us mathematics. It was a daunting subject, and somehow, she seemed the right fit. She had rules, and you had to follow them.

We could not have it any other way. If you were caught doing something else in her class, you had to stand outside with your books. This was a common punishment meted out by most teachers. Free periods were a great source of fun and entertainment for us because we could go and check on the other classes and find out who was standing out! We used to gossip about the number of students who used to get punished in each class. While some took it as a badge of honor to be outside the class, some were mortified, as any passer-by could watch them being punished. However, there used to be rare instances of students being punished by Shetty Teacher. Even the usual suspects would only be found listening to her with rapt attention. It was not that she was lenient; they simply did not dare to cause trouble.

On this particular day, we had her class after recess. My two friends and I had just finished eating our lunch; I had had *chapatis* and *bhindi sabzi*. We washed our lunch boxes while discussing the delay in the arrival of the monsoon. I remarked, "Why isn't the rainy season here yet? We get to have fun, and if it rains too heavily, we may also get a holiday." My two friends, Praveen and Vinod, nodded as they agreed with me. Praveen added, "Yes. I have a plan for the draining of the rainwater. I still have some water balloons left over from Holi. How about I bring them?"

We were excited at this suggestion, and were grinning when we heard a slight cough. Shetty Teacher was washing her lunchbox beside us. We slinked away immediately with the heat blushing on our cheeks. We were embarrassed and also a bit worried. Vinod said, "It is our bad luck that Shetty Teacher heard us. We are in trouble, especially Praveen and myself." I was taken aback. I remonstrated, "What do you mean by that?" Vinod replied, "You are among the top three rankers in the class. We only have average scores. So, we will be punished the most. You may be reprimanded for keeping bad company." While I did not like how this was phrased, I thought that I might be pardoned for being academically gifted. The bell rang, marking the end of the recess. Shetty Teacher walked in, and the three of us were incredibly nervous. She called out the names from the register. Our names were called, and we answered, marking our presence.

She carried on with the attendance procedure normally. Even as we were on pins and needles, Shetty teacher did not utter a word about the incident. It was forty minutes into the class, and we were now sure that we had been given a pass. Suddenly, she wrote down a new math equation and asked the class if anyone would volunteer to answer the question. I wanted to leave a better impression, and I raised my hand. I did not know the answer, but I wanted to put in the effort. I wanted to show Shetty Teacher that even though I liked fun, I was serious about my academics. She gave me the chalk, and I went to the board.

When I walked to the board and started writing down the equations, I realized that I had walked myself into a cul de sac. I was stumped, and I had no idea how to proceed. Shetty Teacher asked me to return to my seat. She then said that students should step forward only if they knew the answer. My cheeks burned from embarrassment. I felt humiliated, and my pride in my academics was also trampled on.

Before wrapping up the class, Shetty Teacher instructed me to meet her at the end of the day. I received sympathetic looks from my classmates as stories that involved meeting her did not really end well. The rest of the day was spent in fear and embarrassment. I could not really focus on the class as I was worried about the repercussions. However, as the day wore on, I felt slightly belligerent. I felt that Shetty Teacher did not respect my achievements. I always worked hard and never slacked when it came to assignments and tests. It was in this sulky mood that I walked into the staff room to meet her.

Luckily, there were no other teachers to witness my punishment. She made me wait, and every passing moment felt like an eternity. After what seemed like an interminable amount of time, she asked me, "Satish, why do you think I have called you in today?" I shifted my weight from one leg to the other and stuttered, "Because I did not answer the question correctly?" She replied, "No. You took the initiative, and not knowing something is not a sin, especially if you look to address it immediately."

I realized that she probably had called me in to reprimand me for the conversation she had overheard during the lunch hour. So, I asked, "Teacher, is it for the conversation that I had with my friends at lunchbreak?" She shook her head and said, "I did not call you in to lecture you on good behavior. I called you to give you some perspective that you may lack. Tell me, Satish, are you happy with the effort you put in to score good marks?" I nodded. She continued, "Do you know why your lunch conversation was a wrong conversation?" I said, "We are students, and we need to focus on studying."

She shook her head again and said, "Satish, it is not about studying. You should have fun. but it has its own time and place. I remember when you took part in the elocution contest, you spoke on the topic of ambition. You spoke with such verve about your desire to leave a mark in this world. Do you think you are on track to achieve it?" I replied, "Yes, teacher. My grades have never dropped, and I am sincere in my assignments. Even if I stumble, I always look to find the answer. Today I will be focusing on the equation I got wrong in class."

She smiled and said, "That is a good attitude, Satish. However, you are only focusing on one facet here. You are only looking at school as an avenue to get good marks. However, that is not enough to go forward in life. You may be happy with the marks you scored today. However, in the coming years after you clear your matriculation examination, you will have to apply to different colleges. You will find that everybody is not the same. There will be countless people who would have scored better marks than you.

They will also come from far more prestigious schools. What will you do then? You also might come across students with lower grades getting into prestigious colleges because of their rich parents. You will also learn how just the name of a person can make all the difference: Tata or Birla, for instance."

I was at a loss for words. Even as I was digesting what Shetty Teacher told me, she continued, "Satish, you need to remember some things. You do not have a last name that is renowned. You do not come from a rich family. Moreover, you do not have inherited wealth to call upon when things get rough.

There are only three ways out in your case: Do not look to educate yourself just from the perspective of scoring good marks. Look at how you can apply what you learn to your daily life. Educate yourself so that you stand out of the crowd because of your efforts and merit. Educate yourself to be better."

This lesson that I received from Shetty Teacher has stayed with me, and it motivates me even today. She showed me how the bigger world would demand a lot more from me than what I had assumed.

I wanted to be a CEO by the age of 45.

So, why did I want to become a CEO? This ambition can be traced to the first job I held. Shetty teacher's advice had proved to be invaluable in my life. It was as if I was wearing blinkers. I never took a day off. I was told about what it would take to be successful, and I ran with it. I was consistently at the top of my class when it came to studies. However, this does not mean I had become a nerd. I took the lead in volunteering and helped organize events in my school and community. The joy of celebrating these grand celebrations made me want to be a part of the organizing team. I learned how organizers budgeted for food, prizes, and space in an increasingly congested Mumbai. I also learned how delegation and trust worked. At the age of 22, I was sure that I wanted to become a CEO. It was my first day of work at Bayer Agrochemicals. I had gotten the job at the college placement fair.

I remember the day as if it was yesterday. I had to report to the office, which was located at Nariman Point. I had woken up nice and early because I did not want to be late. I took the local train, and as I travelled toward my destination, I saw the difference in the outside world. As I neared my destination, the heights of the buildings increased. The clothing worn by the passengers had changed. I soon stepped out and took a bus to the office. I passed by some of the buildings I had seen only in newspapers, like the Assembly Building. I saw the Indian tricolor fluttering in the sea breeze.

Even though it was hoisted on the roof, the size of the flag was stupendous. For some reason, I felt proud to be an Indian. Then I saw the flawless condition of the roads. I remember thinking that one could not have played *lagori* on these streets. Then I noticed the lush green cover. Even as the huge buildings in all their majesty towered alongside the roads, the roads were actually flanked by trees in full bloom. I was then ushered into one of those glass-faceted buildings. I saw it as a step forward. I had taken my first few steps into the world that I dreamed of belonging to. I would come to learn that the grandeur of the building was not in its edifice or in the splendor of the interiors. I saw the building's tiles made up of black marble and saw that some of the seating arrangements were so luxurious looking that they could have been in a brochure. But the charm in the building came from the view it provided. It was beside the coast and provided one of the best views of the Arabian Sea. I remembered the turquoise waters from my childhood visit.

This view however trumped that memory. The sea was placid and I saw gentle waves wash itself onto the coast. That gorgeous view would provide me with an energy boost many a time during my years at Bayer. However, on that particular day, I was taken by the view. To this day, I have no idea how I spent over 15 minutes looking out toward the sea. It felt like a flash. I was interrupted from my reverie when a person from the Human Resources (HR) Department called out my name. I shook away my awe and looked at the concerned person. She told me that I would get five minutes with the CEO of Bayer India's operations.

I was told that it was a standard operating procedure where every new hire would get a chance to interact with the CEO on their first day. I was delighted with this opportunity. I followed my guide and I was led to a huge corner office. Even before I entered, I could see that the CEO had an unparalleled view of the Arabian Sea. I walked in totally amazed by the layout of the office. Perhaps it was because I was so taken by the layout and the view that I had not yet noticed the CEO. He stood up and smiled. He put his hand out and said, "You must be Satish! I know it is a spectacular view. Work hard and it may be yours one day." It was then that I noticed that he was not an Indian.

He was a German. He then introduced himself and we had a lovely chat for about 10 minutes. I was humbled by his openness and warmth. He welcomed me to the company and asked me some questions about myself. I was then directed to my seat. I introduced myself to my new team members and learnt that my neighbor was also a new hire. We both talked of the view, and during a break I raised a question: "Ajay, why do you think a company functioning in India has a German CEO? Why would not they hire an Indian for the task?" Ajay had a small smile and said, "Well, genius! Bayer is a German company. Why would not they hire a German to run the operations in India?" We had a small back-and-forth and both of us even jokingly claimed that we would take that spot someday.

However, it was in the evening when I was returning home that I contemplated the situation. I do not want to sound jingoistic, but I saw the flag on the roof of the Assembly Building once again. It was a strange circumstance as there was no breeze and the flag seemed limp and almost draped around the pole. It was not fluttering proudly as it was in the morning. My thoughts turned toward Bayer and I wondered why they would not hire an Indian to run their operations in India. I felt a burning sense of humiliation. I thought to myself, "Are we as Indians so bad that we need someone else to tell us how to run a company? Is it because of a lack of skill?" I remembered Shetty Teacher's advice. The world had just become a lot bigger to me. So, what if I came from a chawl?

I wanted to be a CEO by the age of 45.

I decided to work hard and constantly look to improve myself. There was this desire in me that would melt all my weariness off. I hustled and looked to learn from every successful deal I clinched or failure I experienced. Five eventful years passed and I was getting noticed. I was getting noticed not just in my company but also from the outside. I was at an industry convention when one man walked up to my table. He introduced himself and asked if I was interested in an opportunity. I immediately saw an opportunity to clinch a new deal.

Before I could say anything, he told me that he was from McCormick and he had a job opening for me. I was stunned. McCormick was one of the biggest US-based multinational companies in the food industry. I was told that they wanted to plant their flag in India. I am sure my eyes lit up when I was told of the opportunity. I took a sip of water to calm my excitement. I do not know why but that water seemed the sweetest that I had ever tasted. I asked for some time to make a decision. I was given time till the end of the week and the person left his contact card with me. That evening I discussed it with my wife. We weighed our options. Although Bayer was much more stable, there was no clear path up the ladder. However, it was an organization that was firmly established and would not be at risk of failure. But this conversation with my wife reminded me of my desire to be a CEO by the age of 45. I picked up the card and dialed the number using my landline. I told this person that I was excited for the adventure.

However, I would realize the scale of the challenge only when I officially joined McCormick. I was their first employee in India. They were still testing the waters and were not ready to commit fully into the project. I was going to be a part of a very small core team to launch the company in India. If our efforts were successful, then the company planned to expand their operations. In essence, this was a real 'start-up', 30 years before it became part of the corporate lexicon.

I helped in hiring a few like-minded and ambitious people to the company. Due to the smaller team and budget, we all had to play multiple roles. One day, I would have to go out and get tea for my team members as they researched and planned for our launch. Another day, I would have to come early to get on a conference call with the senior leadership in McCormick based in the United States of America (USA). So, on that day, I would sweep and clean the office before my team members walked in. They too took turns to perform similar seemingly menial tasks. However, we honored each task with pride. They were essential tasks that needed to be done for a more efficient and effective work force. I assumed the roles of Vice President, Operations Director, Peon, Sweeper, etc., based on the circumstances. I learnt from every role.

If I had to get tea for the team, I had to know where I could get the best tea for the best price. When I had to sweep and mop, I learnt the importance of organization, especially at the end of the day. I learnt the way decisions had to be taken; I had to go to select sites for offices, warehouses, suppliers, etc. None of these tasks bothered me. Shetty Teacher's words resounded in my head. I saw every day as a day to learn something new. It was how I would learn to stand alone from the rest of the pack.

I wanted to be a CEO by the age of 45.

In a story I will recount later, we sadly did not make the impact we had hoped for. McCormick decided to fold its operations in India. They did approach me though, and tell me that they were impressed and happy with my work. While it was a consolation, I was not happy as I had 'failed' in my effort to plant McCormick's flag in India. They then intimated that they had an opening for the position of Marketing Director. I was happy on hearing that I still had a role in the company. I thought of the possibility of moving to the USA as many Indians were doing the same. The IT boom was on its way and people were already moving west to Europe and America for better opportunities.

However, all these dreams and possibilities were brought to a screeching halt when I was informed that the position was in China. I again decided to consult the wisdom of my wife. We also had a young daughter and this was a challenge unlike any other. We again determined the pros and cons of such a move. It would be a risk to move east when everyone else was going west. I will talk more about this later. I remembered my desire and I knew that going to China would teach me more than I would probably learn in any other place. So, I embraced the risk and moved to China with my family. I faced a different set of challenges in China. I had analyzed the failure we experienced in India and learnt lessons from it, and I continued to learn something new every day in China. I separated myself from the rest of the pack. The world had become bigger once again. I would eventually work for six years in Shanghai, and McCormick went from strength to strength during that time.

At the end of six years, McCormick decided that my talents could be better utilized in the USA, and I was soon transferred to the US Headquarters of the company. But still:

I wanted to be a CEO by the age of 45.

I always remembered what Shetty Teacher had told me. Educate yourself. So how do you educate yourself? You can only do so when you consciously put yourself in avenues where you can learn. You have to be willing to risk something to gain something. I took that risk when I went to China. Only by taking risks and learning was I able to separate myself from the pack. When I was moved to the USA, I took a risk on Simply Asia Foods. It is a Thai brand marketed specifically for the American market. At that point, it was not delivering desired results for McCormick. The plan was for McCormick to divest and sell it. However, I saw an opportunity. Most of my work thus far had involved marketing, be it at Bayer, or with McCormick in India and China. If I wanted to be a CEO, I knew that I had to broaden my exposure to different management roles in the company. I had to challenge myself and learn new things.

Even as the consensus was to sell Simply Asia Foods, I wanted it to stay. So, I walked up to the office of the President of McCormick. We were on good personal terms and he welcomed me in and asked, "Well Satish, what can I do for you?" I told him, "Sir, I think selling Simply Asia Foods may turn out to be a mistake. I think there is tremendous untapped potential within that brand and its products." He smiled and said that he recognized that there could be an opportunity. But he clarified, "Satish, there could be potential. However, we cannot simply work on hope and we have tried long enough to make it work. But despite repeated efforts, we have not been able to resuscitate it." I simply stated, "Give me the chance, sir. I will make it work." I could tell that he was surprised at my determination. He held my gaze for a few more seconds. I think he was trying to confirm if I really did have the stomach for the fight. He then simply said, "One year. I will give you one year. If you can turn it around, I will be very happy.

However, you should know, Satish, that this will cost money and time and other resources which could be used elsewhere. You may have to pay the price." I was undaunted. I accepted the challenge undeterred by the prospect of getting fired. This was one of the most intense projects I had ever undertaken and it was also the most formidable. It was even more daunting than the Chinese project. Six months in, the sales graph still had not been corrected. I even entertained second thoughts about the risk I had taken.

Forget becoming a CEO; I now began to have concerns regarding my prospects in my current job position. There was only one solution. I disregarded these thoughts as they were not helping me in any way. I rolled up my sleeves and refocused on things needed to revive Simply Asia Foods.

One-and-half years later, the business started growing well. The much anticipated 'Turnaround' happened. McCormick President Alan Wilson remarked that he had never been more excited about this brand. Today, Simply Asia Foods has been earmarked by McCormick as one of its star products.

I wanted to be a CEO by the age of 45.

My success with Simply Asia Foods only emboldened me to take another risk. I wanted to return to a scene of failure and rectify the error. I wanted to adopt all that I had learned to plant McCormick's flag in India. I discussed and negotiated with the senior leadership to revisit the Indian project. Soon, I turned 45. Was I a CEO yet? No.

But six months after my 45th birthday, McCormick acquired a food company in India and wanted a CEO for its Indian operations. You know where this is going. They did not look for an American to run the entity. They looked to me to head operations in India as Managing Director. I had no bankable last name and my father had no wealth to bequeath, just character. I came from a chawl with an aim to become a CEO by the age of 45.

I was finally a CEO at the age of 45 years and six months.

This is my story of how I had an aspiration and worked toward it. I rolled up my sleeves and worked hard. I looked to learn and still do so. If you want to be anything in life, remember that it does not matter where you come from. What matters is where you want to go. What matters is how badly you want to reach your destination.

Have you heard of the four-minute mile barrier? A mile is the equivalent of 1.6 kilometers. During the mid-point of the last century, there was a lot of upheaval. The two world wars were over. There was the advent of new nations that had carved out their independence from foreign colonists. However, there was one human endeavor that had captured the attention of the world.

It was to see if man could run the mile in under four minutes. There were many efforts to breach that barrier. But no one succeeded in accomplishing that feat. It was at this time the bio-mechanists, physiotherapists, and doctors of that age came up with the suggestion that it was impossible. They contended that the human body was not designed to reach and sustain the speed required to run the mile in under four minutes.

If you want to be technical about it, the speed translates to 15 miles per hour or 24 kilometers per hour. It might not seem all that fast. You may even mistake it for the slow burn pace of the morning rush hour traffic. But at that time, it seemed unfathomable.

The date was May 6, 1954. Three men lined up at the Iffley Road Track at Oxford University. Chris Chataway and Chris Brasher had lined up as pace-setters for a 25-year-old man. Quite ironically, considering the events that would follow, this 25-year-old man was a student studying medicine. His name was Roger Bannister. He would run the mile in 3 minutes and 59.4 seconds. He would repeat the feat two months later, at the 1954 British Empire and Commonwealth Games. Since that fateful day, over 1400 male athletes have breached that barrier.

In fact, John Walker, a New Zealander, ran the mile in under 3 minutes and 50 seconds with a time of 3 minutes and 49.4 seconds. The current fastest mile record is held by a Moroccan, Hicham El Guerroj, who ran the mile in 3 minutes and 43.13 seconds in 1999.

These men scoffed at the idea of the impossible. They ran the mile under 4 minutes and then some. I came from the chawl, but that did not hold me back. I was determined to achieve my goal. I am reminded of a great quote by Muhammad Ali, the legendary boxer. It is filled with such inspiration that it is worth quoting here: "Impossible is just a big word thrown around by small men who find it easier to live in the world they've been given than to explore the power they have to change it. Impossible is not a fact. It's an opinion. Impossible is not a declaration. It's a dare. Impossible is potential. Impossible is temporary. Impossible is nothing."

Adidas would run with the tagline 'Impossible Is Nothing' to great success. However, this phrase is more than just a marketing gimmick. There are lessons to be learnt here. Do not take it only in the literal or pedantic way. I want you to read that quote once again. What do you think Ali is hinting at? Do not be swayed by the literal meaning of the words. What he is indicating is the mentality one needs to adopt. Ali was driven by his need to be the best heavyweight boxer in the world.

That is what I want you to think about. Having dreams is easy. Having ambition is excellent. But they are all just the beginning of the journey. Remember, when you have to climb up a ladder to scale new heights, you always start at the bottom-most rung. Your mentality is what drives you up that ladder. Only when you cultivate the mindset to pursue your goals will you be able to stay on track.

I had the aspiration to be a CEO by the age of 45. What is yours? Think and reflect on it. It is easy to coast along. But if you want to live a remarkable life, it is vital that you define your aspirations. Simply put, figure out what you want to achieve in life. When you figure it out, your actions and attitudes will change due to your set mindset. Aspirations grant you a purpose and a reason to fight and strive in your life.

So how do you figure out your aspirations? The best way is to figure it out for yourself. Draw up a SWOT (Strength, Weakness, Opportunity, and Threat) analysis of yourself. Reflect on your wants and desires. Do not choose transient and short-term wants. Choose an aspiration that will sustain you for the longer term.

Only you can decide this. Some of us make the mistake of fixing our aspirations based on what other people are doing. You see your friends and colleagues do something, and you want to try it too. FOMO, or the fear of missing out, is the wrong way to address life.

Such shared aspirations will never last as they are not what you truly want. Of course, you could ask for guidance to help set your aspirations. You could approach people you respect for advice and set long-term aspirations for yourself. And it is important maintain such relationships even with the passage of time, as they will prove invaluable to you.

Chasing your aspirations can be tough. They test your spirit and mettle every day. Life is never about sailing in the plain sea. You will face storms that will demand your best, even on your worst days. You will face roadblocks, detours, and accidents. How driven will you be when you face these challenges? Sometimes it is not the tough times that will hold us back. Life is not all about thorns; sometimes you get the roses as well.

You will receive unexpected assistance, which will be just as circumstantial as the bad events. Will you become complacent when you receive such good things? Whatever the occasion, you will soon realize that the only thing under your control is the effort you are putting in. Chasing a dream is never easy.

"Press on. Nothing in the world can take the place of persistence. Talent will not; nothing is more common than unsuccessful men with talent. Genius will not; the world is full of educated derelicts. Persistence and determination alone are omnipotent."
– Calvin Coolidge

"When you reach an obstacle, turn it into an opportunity.
You have the choice. You can overcome and be a winner, or you can allow it to overcome you and be a loser.
The choice is yours and yours alone. Refuse to throw in the towel.
Go that extra mile that failures refuse to travel. It is far better to be exhausted from success than to be rested from failure."
– Mary Kay Ash

There are many stages of aspiration. They are closely related to your age. The first stage is your youth. This is when you possess unlimited drive and energy. Fear is a minor factor. You can pursue your goals freely as if you have nothing to lose. The critical thing to do during this stage is to identify your weaknesses. Actively look for opportunities to bolster these weaknesses. Do not let your ignorance and lack of knowledge hold you back. Most often, it is your reluctance and worthless pride that will hold you back at this stage. Dare where others fear. Learn where others play safe. The second stage comes with responsibility. This stage begins when you face the world with the burden of responsibility. You may find yourself married or suddenly find yourself handling something bigger than you are used to. You will find that you no longer have the same dynamism of youth. Your drive is no longer unfettered. You no longer have the same parental safety net underneath.

You will have more familial responsibilities. You will have to plan budgets and pay rents or mortgages. You will increasingly hear terms like work–life balance at this stage. This is the stage where it is easy to give up.

But if you persevere at this stage and not give up on your aspirations, you will soon find your second wind. I am sure you have heard of the term mid-life crisis. Some people distract themselves by buying a new flashy car or some other material things. But what is needed is to refocus. You need to reflect on your aspirations once again, and align them to your current circumstances. Find your footing again. Go up to the attic and find your running shoes. It is time to chase anew.

When you do this, you will get back the same energy and dynamism that you thought you had lost along with your youth. Chasing your dreams is never easy. It will demand the utmost from you, and when you feel that you have given it all you have, it will ask for more.

"You can either choose to wait around and hope life gives you what you want — or you can choose to jump up and put in the work to make your dream come true."
— Oscar Auliq-Ice

"-I suppose it starts with having a dream. And then chasing it. You chase after it like your life depends on it. In a sense, I guess it does.
-What sort of dream?
-Any sort. It doesn't matter what it is.
The only thing that matters is that you want it from the deepest part of who you are, and you chase after it with everything in you."
— Preston Norton, Neanderthal Opens the Door to the Universe

There are a few things I want to you remember. Find your aspirations. Do not let your background or your perceived shortcomings limit you. As Shetty Teacher had advised, "educate, educate, educate" yourself. Never stop learning. Work hard. Do not base your life on the expectations and aspirations of others.

Keep in touch with your aspirations always. Even when life seems down and it is easier to rest, keep your goals in sight. Just as you do not let your background dictate your aspirations, do not let your age make you forget it. There is one final thing that I want to say: always marry your aspirations to your values. There is only one thing that you should never compromise on in the pursuit of your dreams—your set of values. We shall discuss more on that in the next chapter. So, I went from a chawl to be a CEO. Where will you go?

2

PASSION AND ENTHUSIASM

"There is a real magic in enthusiasm. It spells the difference between mediocrity and accomplishment."
– Norman Vincent Peale.

There might not be two more oft-used words than passion and enthusiasm. People tend to use them as buzz phrases without ever thinking about what they entail. There are cliched sayings of how living a life of passion and enthusiasm is the best way to live life. Let us first begin by trying to define passion and enthusiasm. If we were to consult the Oxford dictionary, we would find that passion is defined as *'a strong and barely controllable emotion.'* Enthusiasm, meanwhile, is defined as *'intense and eager enjoyment, interest, or approval.'* Of course, these definitions are the most basic steps in trying to understand what these two words mean. We also need to figure out how they fit within the context of our lives.

Passion, for me, is about purpose. If you want to do something and you are passionate about it, you will find that the fire will continually burn within you.

Even if you achieve a certain goal, you will find that your embers have not been doused. Look at some of the great cricketers from India, be it Sachin Tendulkar or Virat Kohli. They are incredibly passionate about their craft.

Even as they made a prodigious number of runs and numerous records tumbled down, they kept on persevering. It was the drive to be the best run-getter that drove them. It was this desire that made Virat shift from a meat-based diet to a plant-based diet. He gave up the delicacies he grew up eating. He realized that good nutrition was essential to his physical fitness, which would help him perform better. Enthusiasm, on the other hand, I believe is more of a short-term burst. It can provide you with an intense desire to do something. However, the fatal weakness of enthusiasm is that it is often not paired with a purpose. When it is not allied thus, you will find that your enthusiasm will run out when confronted by the inevitable challenges. At its core, both passion and enthusiasm will drive you forward. They are both essential to make something out of your life. Passion gives you the direction and destination; enthusiasm keeps you on the road to reaching that destination.

"It is obvious that we can no more explain a passion to a person who has never experienced it than we can explain light to the blind."
– T. S. Eliot

When people think of passion, they generally only think of the result of that passion. But passion is a far more demanding emotion than one would imagine. It will ask for your effort, and it will not be bowed down by suffering. To find out if you are truly passionate about something, find out how obsessed you are with it. Let us say you are training for a marathon. When people ask why you are training for such an event that demands great endurance, you reply by saying that you are passionate about running. However, you may change your stance, once you experience real pain at the end of the first training session. You may sprain an ankle. You may even suffer from some cramps.

You will be unbelievably exhausted at the end of it. You may not even hit your targets for the first training session. You may have found that the energy you had started out with was drained by the copious amount of sweat early in the session. If you curse and quit, then running was never your passion.

Maybe it was the photographs or the medals that you craved. If you are truly passionate about running, you would have contacted other marathon runners and asked for their advice. You would have read up and improved your knowledge on topics like hydration and nutrition to help you run that marathon. You would find yourself trying to think of ways to convert that pain into pleasure. You would find yourself pushing yourself a little bit more every training session.

It can be annoying when you keep hearing the word passion as a buzzword. Every motivational speaker or video will harp on the importance of this word. They will recount the many examples of successful people who achieved their goals because of their passion. Here is the key detail about passion that you should know. Passion gets you excited about life. Why? Passion points to the life that *you* want to live. It does not point to the life that your parents want for you or what society deems fit for you. It is your life.

Enthusiasm is about the inner energy which makes you charge forward. When you are enthusiastic about something you are truly passionate about, it would be like rolling a stone down a cliff. You will respond more positively, and you will accumulate more energy as you go along. A commonly misused word interchangeable with passion is motivation. Motivation is about finding the inner drive to do something worthwhile. It is more personal as it demands that you reflect on what you truly want. Enthusiasm is more about the inner strength to address an immediate lack. Let us take a basic example. Let us say you want to lose weight. You probably will find the enthusiasm to go to a gym for a few days or weeks.

However, you will stop in your efforts after a few days when it is not driven by a personal need to lose weight. You can try and find many motivational videos on YouTube to help you with your motivation.

However, they might or might not be of use to you as they are made for a general audience. You will need to reflect on why you truly want to lose weight if you want to find your motivation. If you are only looking to lose weight to fit into an image suggested by society, your challenge would only get harder. I am sure many of you would have heard enough people tell you that you should follow your passion.

However, this is easier said than done. Most people are not sure what their passion is. They do not know how to identify their passion. There may be activities that people like doing, but they cannot be sure if it is a hobby or a passion. If you find yourself stuck in a similar rut, I have some tips for you. Take your time and truly reflect on these steps. The first step in finding your passion is having the right mentality. If you proceed with the mindset that finding your passion is going to be difficult, I have news for you. It is certainly going to be difficult with a defeatist attitude.

Take the instance when you decide to watch a movie in a theatre with your friends. You want to watch an action film, but the majority of your friends decide to watch a horror film instead. As you walk to your seat in the theatre you will be filled with the negative feeling that you do not want to watch this movie You may even be thinking that you do not want to be there at all.

Thus, even before the film begins, you would have made yourself uncomfortable, and even if the film was exceptionally entertaining, you will never be able to truly enjoy the experience. This attitude applies to the exercise of finding your passion as well. If you think it is going to be hard, you are already tainting the process with your prejudice. You will never truly find your passion as you would have closed your mind to the possibilities.

"Always remember, you have within you the strength, the patience, and the
passion to reach for the stars to change the world."
– Harriet Tubman

The second step would be to identify the zircons from the diamonds in your life. Do not be confused about what you are truly passionate about. You could have many interests. Let us say you enjoy an activity where you help people speak better. You may think that helping others find happiness might be your true passion. However, this would be after just a surface-level examination. Probe deeper, and you may find that your true passion lies in leadership within your community. It is not a hard and fast rule that leadership is what drives you in the case. As I mentioned earlier, I want you to be open to all possibilities. Put your treasured memories and highs under the microscope and ask yourself what you are truly passionate about.

You may now tell me that you have diverse interests that stretch from Kashmir to Kanyakumari. Imagine you are a chef. You open a pantry and find ingredients from fish and meats to chocolates and ice cream, and you are being asked to cook a single dish without any pointers. This can be confusing. When you find yourself in such a situation, look for the commonality in all your interests. If you think of activities stretching from Kashmir to Kanyakumari, the obvious commonality is India. While this example is a bit oversimplified, the idea is the same. You need to look at the broader picture and find what unites all your interests. Let us say you are interested in things like anime to video games, and films. You could say they all fall under the umbrella of entertainment. However, there is more when you look deeper. Is it the storytelling that interests you? Or is it the animation or visual style that you are interested in?

The next step is the most crucial one. You need to distinguish between a hobby and a job that helps you make money. You will find that turning hobbies into an income-earning activity is a lot tougher than you can imagine. You may find that a certain activity fills you with great pleasure. It makes you look forward to the next day. Now you have to ask yourself a couple of questions: Who are the people who would benefit from this particular activity and how can I reach them? Let us suppose that you are passionate about being a writer.

You will soon find out that there are a few allied skills that you would need. And to pick up these required skills, you could take up working in some related field. To be successful in a writing career, you could become a journalist and learn a few skills. You may have to learn how to frame an interview and write in shorthand, or you may acquire design skills for a newspaper print.

If you become a content writer, you may have to learn about SEO and how your content needs to be tailored along those specific terms. The best way to address this issue is to reach out to people you admire and look up to, who are in your line of passion, and ask them for advice. Aim to have a conversation with them and find out how you can transform your passion into profit. When you pursue your passion, you will find that you are challenged from within and around you.

I am sure you have heard of the film Gully Boy. People will not believe that you can make it when you chase your passion. Brodha V is one of the foremost Indian rappers who raps in English. In some of his songs, he details how people mocked him for his choice to be a rapper. He also talks of how people tried to pressure his parents about his career choice. Criticizing voices can be cacophonous, and damaging too, if you allow them to plant a seed of doubt in your mind. This constantly makes you doubt yourself and second-guess yourself. I am not asking you to ignore such people, especially if they are family members. They voice their doubts due to their concern for you. If you are sure of your passion, then ignore their complaints. Find your own voice to help soothe the complaints.

The most crucial ingredient in chasing your passion is your bravery. Brené Brown said it best: *"You can choose courage, or you can choose comfort, but you cannot choose both."* Chasing your passion may lead you to quit a high-paying job. You should be ready to face the challenges that will be thrown at you. However, when you have identified your passion, you will be clear about the path you have to take. What matters is whether you have the perseverance to stay on the path. You need an investigation into your passion.

You could say that you like watching movies on your couch. Then find out what it is about movies that catches your interest? Is it the acting? Is it the story? Or is it the way the director tells the story? Reflect on what you would like to do. If it is acting, then find some way to get an acting role. I am not asking you to audition for a blockbuster role. You can start small by auditioning for local stage plays.

Work on your craft and look to improve. If you look at the journeys of some of the finest actors in India or abroad, you will find that they all have their roots in theatre. I want to warn you that your passion needs nurturing to keep the fire going. Do not think that once you have identified your passion, it will remain static. Along with your passion, it takes relentless pursuit and perseverance to achieve your goals. Two of the most iconic basketball players who dominated the game after Michael Jordan were Allen Iverson and Kobe Bryant.

Their passion for the sport drove them both. Iverson came into a physical league that big men dominated. Iverson was only 6 feet tall, a veritable smaller guard when people who played in his position were much taller. But his mesmerizing dribbles and crossovers tripped the best of defenders. He became an inspiration and an icon for many basketball players in the years to come. However, Iverson never won a National Basketball Association (NBA) title. Bryant won five titles. He, too, was a dominant guard like Iverson. They even clashed once in one of the most iconic NBA finals in 2001. At that point, Iverson was considered a far superior player. He had carried the team single-handedly into the finals. Bryant, meanwhile, came into the final in the company of another superstar, Shaquille O'Neal. But Iverson put up a dominant display in the first game of the series with his customary swagger and style to lead his team to victory. Bryant and O'Neal closed out the series from there. If you were to look back at their legacies, Bryant is considered one of the most iconic champions, well renowned for his work ethic and study. Iverson, while having a spectacular career, is not held in the same regard.

Iverson would tell a story later, which would reflect on their difference. Iverson came to Los Angeles for the off-season. He wanted to hit the clubs and have a bit of fun after a long season. He called Bryant and asked if he had the time to show him around as Bryant's team was based in Los Angeles. Kobe received him at the airport and they had lunch together. Then he drove him to Iverson's hotel. Iverson was confused as this was not a club where he could party with Bryant. Bryant remarked that this was where he would stop. He had to go back to the gym for practice. He did not take a day off. A day not spent playing was spent on how he could improve his game. It is one of the greatest examples of how simply being passionate is not enough to be successful. You need to grow your passion to the extent of obsession. Always look for ways to improve, because there is no such thing as perfection. So, there will always be some detail that needs to be straightened out or worked upon. Passion requires an obsessive commitment to hone and improve oneself. You will find many inspiring speeches on YouTube by many luminaries.

I urge you to listen to Steve Jobs's speech at the Stanford commencement from 2005. He talked about three stories in the speech, which can help distill the points I wish to make. The first story he talked of is of how dots can be connected. He began by saying how he was adopted by his parents, who promised his birth mother that he would get a college education. But Jobs dropped out of college in six months. He would occasionally drop in on various classes. Jobs said that he never understood the value of a college education. He saw that his parents were spending their life savings on an expensive college course in which he saw no value. He added that one of the classes that he had dropped in was a calligraphy class. He was fascinated with the style and beauty of it. He found that class interesting, but it had no practical application in real life. Ten years later, when they were designing the first Macintosh, all his calligraphy lessons came rushing back to him. So, he built the typography into the computer. Jobs remarks that these dots only connected ten years after the class.

So, do what you are passionate about even when you have no immediate result. Patience is another virtue that will help you keep your ship on an even keel even when confronted by the violent waves of reality.

"So, you have to trust that the dots will somehow connect in your future. You have to trust in something, your gut, destiny, life, karma, whatever. Because believing that the dots will connect down the road will give you the confidence to follow your heart even when it leads you off the well-worn path and that will make all the difference."
— Steve Jobs

His second story was about love and loss. He talked of how he loved what he did and how that translated into converting Apple from a two-man operation from a garage to a 2-billion-dollar company with over 4,000 employees. However, he was soon fired from the company. He talked of how he felt lost, and it was the reminder that he still loved what he did that gave him the desire to stay in Silicon Valley and start NeXT and Pixar.

He then returned to Apple when it acquired NeXT and used his work at NeXT to drive the renaissance at Apple.

"I had been rejected, but I was still in love." — Steve Jobs.

It was this passion that helped him tide over being a public failure. It was this passion that helped him move on and come back stronger. His third story was about death. He started by recounting a quote: *"If you live each day as if it was your last, someday you'll most certainly be right."* He talked of how that made an impression on him and how every morning he would stand in front of the mirror and ask himself, *"If today were the last day of my life, would I want to do what I am about to do today?"* It was how he kept track of his passion. Whenever he found that the answer was a 'No' for several days, he knew that he had to change something.

"Remembering that you are going to die is the best way I know to avoid the trap of thinking you have something to lose. You are already naked. There is no reason not to follow your heart."
– Steve Jobs

He then talked of how his cancer diagnosis changed his entire perspective on life. He was told that he would only have six months to live, and sometime later, after they did a biopsy, they informed him that his cancer was treatable with surgery. He then talked of how death is a destination we all share, even when none of us actually wants to die. He talked of death as the greatest invention of life as it clears the old to make place for the new. He then exhorted his audience that their time was limited and told them not to waste it by living someone else's life. Jobs' mirror test will help you bring focus to your daily tasks. It will remind you to keep your fires stoked and burning. (I, too, have a mirror test. It was prescribed to me by my father. We shall cover that later.) If I were to sum up my insights into passion and enthusiasm, I would ask you to take your time to reflect on it.

The chances are that you already know what your passion is; it could be that you are simply ignoring the possibilities. If you ever find yourself dreading the day or living the weekday in anticipation of the weekend, you are wasting your life and potential. The world needs your energy and drive. So, put your likes and interests under the scanner. Probe them deeply and find what your passion is. If you like reading books, think about opening a book store or a library.

Find ways to connect with people. Start a subscription service for like-minded people. Send them books and spread your joy with them. When you know for sure what you are passionate about, know that you are ahead of many who have not even taken the first step like you. Whenever I found myself passionate about something, I would spend a lot of time just digging around for information. Once upon a time, it was through books. With the advent of Google, this process has become simpler. Passionate people will spend a lot of time on their passions.

So, chart your days and find out what takes up most of your time. The chances are that your passion will stare back at you from the black-and-white chart. It is important that you question people around you to find out what needs to be done. There are forums that can provide mentorships to people who need them. If you are a woman and want mentorship in journalism, there is the forum, Digital Women Leaders, where accomplished women journalists provide one-on-one mentorship. Attend workshops that cater to your passions. I had said earlier that sometimes you might have to quit your job. However, I caution you not to take that leap until you are very sure. You could begin by experimenting with your interests as a hobby. Find out if it is viable and not; then find out where your deficiencies lie and address them.

"Twenty years from now, you will be more disappointed by the things that you didn't do than by the ones you did do. So, throw off the bowlines.
Sail away from the safe harbor.
Catch the trade winds in your sails.
Explore. Dream. Discover."
– Mark Twain

PART B: THE RECIPE FOR A QUALITY LIFE

3

THE LICENSE TO LIVE AS A
HUMAN BEING

"It's like, at the end, there's this surprise quiz: Am I proud of me? I gave my life to become the person I am right now. Was it worth what I paid?"
— Richard Bach

Let us begin with an analogy. Assume you are the captain of a ship. You are sailing in unexplored waters in search of land. It is dark, and you have no map to help you navigate. You have only heard legends of monsters, shipwrecks, and storms in this part of the world. Your crew depends on you to keep them safe. Suddenly, you see a beacon of light. It is a lighthouse. You know that you are safe now.

Similarly, when you navigate your way in life, there will be moments when you feel lost. It is at such junctures that your values illuminate your way forward. This is why companies and educational institutions paint their values on their walls. So, when you enter their premises, you know what they stand for.

Your values must be immutable and firm and should never be dependent upon any context. They are the guiding markers that highlight the correct way forward. If you were to Google the word *values*, you would find over 900 million results. There are many abstract theories and concepts related to the word. Whatever be the case, there is always a moral implication. In the last chapter, I let you know about the importance of aspirations. But in this chapter, I want to talk about *how* you achieve those aspirations. If you were to ask me about three values that should never be compromised upon, I would say they are honesty, integrity, and empathy.

Honesty and integrity can not only be your individual qualities, but they also can play a pivotal role in building trust and confidence in your interactions and relationships with others. Let us first understand the difference between the two. Honesty is about being truthful, fair, and just. Integrity is about your commitment to adhere to high moral standards even in the face of extremely trying circumstances. Honesty is the bedrock on which you cultivate your integrity.

I would like to return to a tale from my childhood. This is a story about Mr. Yadav. Mr. Yadav, as I told you before, was one of the most esteemed members of my society. If Raymond ever looked for a model for the 'Complete Man' commercial in my neighborhood, Mr. Yadav would have been the obvious choice for the role. It was clear from the way he dressed. His dresses were immaculate and always stood out. His clothes were always neatly ironed. His hair was well-coiffed. His shoes always sparkled with the polish he applied every day.

His family members, too, were always decked out in the finest clothes; you would never see them wearing any hand-me-downs. He was one of the most educated people in the community. He had received a college education, and he got his degree certificate framed and hung it up in his living hall. It was a symbol of his excellence. In a colony full of workers and laborers, he was among the rare few who were at the management level. However, he was never standoffish. He would welcome all of us to his house.

We used to watch cricket matches at his home as he was the only one in the entire building who owned a television set. His hospitality and warmth, along with his education and sophistication, meant that he was one of the pillars of my community. He was an officer in a leading automobile company and was well regarded.

He was so widely respected that the members of my society had unanimously elected him as the Secretary of the Association. He also functioned as the treasurer for our community. I am sure you must be familiar with the term 'maintenance fees.' Mr. Yadav collected fees from the members of our community for that purpose. All of us used to contribute money. He repurposed this money in a variety of ways. He used to set aside some money for celebrations and festivals. He used the money to buy the Ganesh idol for Ganesh Chaturthi. He also made catering arrangements to provide food for the community.

He was also a key member of the planning committee for these events. He never spared any expense when it came to the celebrations in our society. Each event felt like a grand celebration, and it always brought the whole society together. We had occasions where the Muslim members of the community would celebrate Diwali with us, and we would celebrate Eid with them. As my family and I were vegetarians, we refrained from consuming the food, but we always wished them well and ate some sweets. We were as close-knit as a community could be.

Mr. Yadav also had another purpose for the money. He was supposed to save some money every month and deposit it in a bank account. It was supposed to be a rainy day fund for the community. He maintained the bank account, and none of the society members ever quizzed him about it. We had such unshakeable trust in him. So, we never asked him to produce the passbook or any financial statement to keep track of the account. I clearly remember this particular day. One of the members of our colony met with an accident. He was the sole breadwinner of his family. They did not have enough money to pay for the hospital expenses. Mr. Yadav was out on a business trip.

The members of the society came together and decided that the emergency fund should be used to help the concerned family. My father and a couple of other men went to Mr. Yadav's house to enquire about his expected arrival and the access to the bank account. I was seven years old at that time. I tagged along with two other boys as our fathers went to Mr. Yadav's residence. His wife answered the door and served us all tea.

After the pleasantries were dealt with, my father asked, "Madam, when is Mr. Yadav expected back?" He then went on to explain the situation. She paled and said that her husband would be returning at night. When enquired about the bank account, she said, "Please ask my husband about it. I am not really sure of the details."

We were then slowly ushered out. I looked at my father and the other men. Their faces seemed to be set in granite. Their jaws were clenched, and it did seem like they were a bit angry and disappointed. I never understood their expressions that night. The following day was a Sunday. Some of us children were playing on the road when we saw a lot of adults walking toward my home. They all seemed angry, and I was yet to realize the gravity of the situation. Then I saw that Mr. Yadav's scooter was parked near the building. My footsteps automatically lead me home. As I climbed the stairs, it was evident that there were a lot of people in my home.

The slippers outside seemed to be discarded haphazardly as if the people inside had much bigger issues to worry about than the safety of their footwear. I found them strewed up to almost a flight of stairs below my floor. I carefully navigated the slippers and the stairs using the balls of my feet. I slowly tiptoed my way into the house. There was a huge crowd, and all of them seemed to be facing the sofa in my house. I peeked through the mass of people. The tension and anger seemed palpable. I saw that the anger was directed at a distraught Mr. Yadav. He was seated on the sofa with my father, who had his arm around him. The man who had hitherto stood tall and erect was now hunched over in anguish. I gathered from the snippets of angry rebukes that he had misappropriated the colony funds for his personal use.

It was only later that the entire matter came to light. Mr. Yadav was used to his luxurious life, and he could not sustain it on his salary alone. In the beginning, he was sincere with the money. He was steadfast in his bookkeeping. However, one day he was tempted to use a small amount of money from the community funds to buy some expensive clothes for his wife. He reimbursed the amount he had withdrawn as soon as he received his salary. No one was any the wiser. He was further emboldened by that getaway. He soon started misusing larger amounts for his personal needs. Since there was no one to oversee his spending, he also began to procrastinate when it came to filling in the missing funds. It would also come to light that he had misappropriated funds by overcharging certain expenses during the festivals to pocket some of the money. The Society only caught on to his misdeeds when we needed that emergency money.

People were surprised and disappointed that an educated man like Mr. Yadav did not know better. He had defrauded them of the money. However, he assured everyone in the community that he would refund the money he had misused. I only realized the gravity of his mistake when Mr. Yadav was forced to sell his house and scooter to refund the money. My lasting memory of him was not of a stalwart man standing tall and smiling, but a person hunched over in shame and repentance with tears in my house. Due to his dishonest behavior, he did not just lose his house; he also lost his standing within the community.

I was very surprised that even a bulwark of the community like Mr. Yadav could have such a steep fall. That evening my father was in a somber mood. He saw me watching him, and he beckoned me over. I sat down next to him and asked, "Father, how did Yadavji fail? He was so generous and welcoming. I also know that he is the only one who is highly educated in our colony. Did they not teach him in his school and college that he should not cheat?" My father brushed my hair, and said, "Education will tell you how to do things and what to do in certain circumstances. For example, if you go to college, you may be taught how to make money. But it is the strength of your character that will tell you how you should not earn money.

It is your moral fiber that will tell you that committing a bad deed is inherently wrong." I asked him, "So how do I ensure that I also do not fall into the same trap?" He replied, "There is one simple method. I call it as a mirror test. Son, every day just before you go to sleep, stand in front of the mirror. Reflect on your day and ask yourself just one question. Have I done anything today that I will be embarrassed or guilty of sharing with others? If you feel that there is something you could not share without feeling those emotions, you will know that you did something wrong. Do not commit those deeds again."

The mirror test echoes the African proverb that a clean conscience is the best pillow. Shetty Teacher may have taught me the importance of education, but my father taught me the importance of living life the right way. You, too, should follow the mirror test.

Ask yourself at the end of every day if you have done anything that inspires feelings of guilt or shame within you. The mirror test forces you to be honest with yourself. It reflects the imperfections in your character. I am sure your parents or grandparents had asked you to be good children even when you felt that nobody was watching. They would have told you that the Gods were watching you. You may no longer be a child, but the mirror test will remind you of one indelible truth. There is always one witness to your actions. That witness is you. You know what you have done, and the mirror test will let you know when you have done something wrong. Integrity is another value that is held as highly as honesty. There is a misconception that these qualities are interchangeable. They are not; you can be honest but have no integrity, but to have integrity, you must be honest. Let me recount a story from my time at Bayer Chemicals. As I had mentioned in the previous chapter, this was my first job. I was from a lower-middle-class family and generally used the local trains to travel within the city of Mumbai. I have told you of my meeting with the CEO on my first day. Later that day, I was asked to head to the HR department. They asked me to fill in a few forms, and then they gave me an offer letter that required my signature for their records.

As I was reading through the letter, I saw a breakdown of my salary. I noticed one item that said daily taxi allowance. Bayer was going to give me rupees 160 per day for my to-and-fro commute to the office. I immediately asked the HR person for the specific details. She said, "Yes, we will provide you with rupees 160 for your travel to the office from your home and back. We will also reimburse any travel expenditures you may accrue for office purposes."

I was shocked and I asked, "How do we redeem the taxi allowance?" She said, "Just let us know at the end of the month. Let us know how many days you availed the taxi, and we will reimburse you with the appropriate amount when you receive your salary." I was shocked at their incentive. I am sure you are surprised as well at the amount! This was a much earlier era, and indicative of the times, there was no system of keeping bills or receipts. We just had to create our own vouchers to redeem the daily taxi allowance. I then discussed this with my colleague, Ajay. I found out that his house was only a couple of train stations away from my house.

Suddenly, I had a brainwave. I told him, "Ajay, just think about it. I spend about rupees 5 per day for my to-and-fro train fare. If I start from home a little earlier, I can walk to the office and still be on time. My house is close to the station, so I can walk that way too. I am sure you are also placed similarly. So, think about it. What if we took the train every day to work, but claimed that we travelled by taxi daily? We will make free money every day. We will make a profit of rupees 155 per day." I could see Ajay was also delighted with the plan. Then he raised a pertinent question, "But what if we are caught?" However, I was slightly blinded by the possibility of making some extra money with a minimal effort. I said, "I am sure they will not check. I asked them about the reimbursement procedure and was told that it is given on a trust basis."

I never realized the weight of the words I had just uttered. I was looking to make money by abusing their trust. Our motivation to make money was also poor. Nariman Point had a few good five-star hotels which served expensive foreign liquor. We wanted to sample that and have a good time.

This extra money would go toward partying and would not compromise our regular salaries. We stuck to the plan and started early every day. We would meet on the same train and then walk to the office together when we alighted from the train. At the end of the month, we went to the HR department and claimed that we had traveled via taxi. To avoid any suspicion, we went on completely different days and at different times. Ajay went to claim his allowance on the morning of the penultimate day of the month.

I went on the evening of the final day of the month. They were gracious and marked it down without any further query. That evening we could not help but laugh at the marvel of our scheme. When we received our salary, we saw that we were indeed 'reimbursed' with the extra money. We could not help but giggle when we saw it. Our office colleagues asked for the reason for our mirth. But we were thick as thieves. We did not want anyone else to make money the same way as then we would all be sure to get caught. However, deep inside, we knew that we could not share our secret scheme because we knew it was wrong.

However, we drowned all our cares that weekend when we went and had fun at the local watering hole. The next day, I was nursing a headache at home. My father came into my room and sat down on my bed. Due to my daily early morning start, I had not had a proper conversation with my him for nearly a month. He was curious about my first month at work. He wanted to know if I was working hard. He was curious about my coworkers and bosses. I told him of the spectacular views from my office building. I told him of my conversation with the CEO. I also remarked how he was not an Indian. I then voiced out my desire to be an Indian CEO for an MNC's operations in India. He was very happy with my aims. As we conversed, I told him of my colleagues. I talked of their professionalism, generosity, and warmth.

Maybe it was because of the comfortable conversation we were having that I told him of the new money-making scheme I had devised. After explaining the ruse in detail, I laughed, "They are such fools.

They just believed me, and I was able to make some money." However, my father's reaction was the opposite of Ajay's reaction. I could see that he was furious. He told me, "I am disappointed in you. Son, I need you to remember one thing. No one made it big by monkeying around, and you are monkeying around." Even as I was stunned, he continued, "I want you to answer me honestly. Will you be able to share this money-making scheme with the finance manager of your company? Will you be able to tell him honestly that the HR people are so stupid that they trust you to be honest?"

His questions struck me with the force of hammer blows. I was mortified. When I answered in the negative, he reminded me of the mirror test. He said, "Do not compromise on your values. Do you remember Mr. Yadav? Do you remember how you wanted to avoid such a fate?" I could only mutely nod. I had no words as the weight of my actions finally made its presence known. He continued, "Like I told you before, at the end of the day, look into the mirror. Ask yourself if you have done anything you cannot share with others because it embarrasses you or makes you feel guilty. If you feel those emotions, you have lost your license to live as a human being."

The last part of that statement might seem like an overkill. But my father always believed that one could do better than what one's baser instincts suggested. It was never a choice when it came to your values. His teachings have remained with me to this day. If our intellect is what separates our species from the others, it is our values that make us human beings. After that incident, I subject myself to the mirror test every day. This rigorous, daily self-examination has meant that even the pressures of running an MNC worth millions of dollars have never affected my sleep. I am not trying to claim that I have not made mistakes and have led a perfect life. But I have been perfectly true to my values. My mistakes have never compromised my values or the values of my organization.

I remember an incident when I returned to run operations for McCormick in India. I was based in Delhi at that time. A business partner had come to my home for Diwali celebrations. Diwali is the festival of lights, crackers, and, more importantly, gifts.

My family had organized a dinner party. We had prepared a sumptuous meal, and we had a good time. We played *Antakshari* and had a good time socializing with one another. The business partner had come to my house with a basket filled with flowers, fruits, dry fruits, etc. It was a veritable feast to the eyes. The basket was wrapped in this beautiful cellophane cover with a beautiful bow tied around it. We, too, had given them a similar basket of fruits, chocolates, and dry fruits. We then watched the lights and fireworks display as the crackers burst in the sky.

We just sat on the balcony and had an amazing view of the various lights and sounds. When the din had finally calmed down, they decided that they could travel back home without disturbance. We made plans to meet regularly, and my wife and I felt that this relationship could extend beyond business and that we all could become good friends.

We bid them goodbye and returned to our house. We saw the gift basket and decided that it was best to sort it out immediately instead of keeping it for the next day. So, we prepared some tea for both of us and started sorting the basket. We saw the quality of the fruits and remarked how fresh they looked. I made a mental note to ask them about their grocer.

We sipped our tea as we separated the fruits, dry fruits, and sundries into different piles. As we were doing this, we came across a gift-wrapped object. The box was rectangular in shape, and the gift-wrapping was immaculate. I removed the wrapper carefully taking care not to disturb the aesthetic beauty of the package. As I removed the wrapper, I could see a pearly white box inside. As I slowly unraveled the wrapping, I saw it was an Apple iPad. I was shocked, and I almost dropped it, and my leg kicked the table. However, my glass of tea hit the table deck due to my sudden impetus. The tea spilled, and the iPad was kept aside. As I was cleaning the table, my mind was slightly muddled with many thoughts. There was a slight inkling that I could keep the iPad. It was the latest iteration of the product. I thought I could give it to my daughter. However, there was a major block to the plan. I knew I should not keep it.

A vagrant thought intervened, "I am the CEO. I have no one to report to, and I am sure no one will know. Only our two families will know. I could keep it." I was not sure what to do as my mind was in conflict. However, I gained clarity when I stood in front of the mirror before I went to sleep. I asked myself, "Satish, is there anything that you did that you would not be able to share with anyone because of shame or guilt?" The answer was seen in stark detail. My company had a policy that stated employees could not receive non-perishable gifts over the value of $20. I do not need to tell you that the iPad's value was way over that limit.

As the CEO, I had to set an example. So, the next day, I called the partner and thanked him for his time. I also thanked him for the fruits and other perishable goods. But I politely explained to him that I had to return the iPad as it would compromise on my values and my company's values. He was shocked that someone would return a Diwali gift. He would later confide that I was the first to return a gift in his entire professional career. Our bond only strengthened after that call. We remain good friends to this day.

Do you know why you should not compromise on honesty and integrity? A lie could help you adjust, but then you will be forever stuck making adjustments. I am sure you are familiar with the fable of the boy who called 'wolf.' People will lose trust in you. More importantly, you will lose trust in yourself. You will know that you cannot rely on yourself. Another damaging consequence is that your words will have no value. Your word should be your bond. If you cannot stand by your own words, what can you stand for?

People often talk of how truth alleviates many burdens. When you lead a life that is low on values, it can get tiring. When you tell lies, you need to prop it up with other lies. The maintenance of this castle of cards can drain you emotionally and mentally. They add unnecessary stress to your life as you are forced to keep up the façade. One of the most damning things you can do to yourself is to compromise on your values. When you do it the first time and accept it, you are subconsciously signaling that it is okay to compromise. You subconsciously signal that you expect little of yourself.

You lower the bar for yourself. When you lower your standards, you will stagnate as you need the stimulus of a higher standard to grow and evolve.

The lasting consequence of lowering your standard is that you leave no legacy. Think of the people whose names are revered and respected. Listen to their words. They never took a day off. There was never a day when they compromised on their values. They strictly regulated their lives based on the morals and values they deemed unshakeable. I came across this wonderful story of a man by the name of Ian Rosenberger.

He was a participant in a competition-based reality show called *Survivor*. He participated in the year 2005. It was the penultimate round, and there were only three contestants left out of the original 20. They were Ian Rosenberger, Katie Gallaher, and Rosenberger's best friend on the show, Tom Westman. The winner of this round would get the opportunity to eliminate one of the other two for the final.

The winner's prize at the end of the show would be one million dollars. The challenge was a test of perseverance and endurance. The contestants had to hang onto a buoy in the ocean. The person who held on for the longest time would be the winner. Ian Rosenberger had been hanging onto the buoy for over 12 hours. Five hours earlier, Katie had dropped out.

As he hung on, Ian realized that he had a clear path for victory. He knew that if he had to win the competition, he had to win this round and eliminate his friend Tom. As Ian hung on, he kept repeating the Scout Law he had learned as a child when he was an Eagle Scout. The Law stresses that a scout is supposed to be trustworthy and loyal.

As he repeated the words, he reflected on his time in the competition. He remembered that the nature of the competition was to eliminate others. How could he be trustworthy and loyal in such a competition? He knew the cost of the million dollars; he would have to eliminate his friend and possibly lose his friendship. So, Ian quit.

He would later remark that even if he had won the million dollars by eliminating his friend, it would not have sat well with him. He knew that the prize money would weigh heavily on his soul. Tom would go on to win the competition. But people always remembered Ian from that year's batch of contestants.

"Empathy is the most mysterious transaction that the human soul can have, and it's accessible to all of us, but we have to give ourselves the opportunity to identify, to plunge ourselves in a story where we see the world from the bottom up or through another's eyes or heart."
– Sue Monk Kidd

There is a story of a farmer who wanted to sell some puppies as his dog had just given birth to a litter. He put up a puppies-for-sale sign and nailed it onto a post. When he finished that job, he felt a tug at his pants. He looked down and saw a young boy looking at him with expectant eyes. He asked if he could buy a puppy. The boy was dressed in neat clothes and seemed sincere. The farmer smiled and said that he needed to be sure that the puppies went to a good home. The boy assured the farmer that his house would be a loving and caring one for the puppy. The farmer then whistled and called out his dog's name. A resounding bark followed. A dog came pelting out of nowhere, followed by four small balls of fur. The puppies looked cute. Suddenly, the boy saw another ball of fur limping behind. He was smaller and was the runt of the litter.

The boy pointed at him and told the farmer that he wanted that puppy. The farmer tried to dissuade him and said, "Son! Trust me. He will never be able to run and frolic around with you. The other puppies are healthy, and you will have a lot more fun with any one of them." The boy smiled and stepped back. He then pulled up one of the legs of his trousers. It revealed a prosthetic leg. He said, "I, too, can't run. He needs someone who will understand." The farmer was stumped. And with tears in his eyes, he took the little puppy and gave it to the young boy. What can you learn from the story? It is about the boy's empathy. I, too, learned a powerful lesson of empathy. I used to visit India for holidays when I lived in the USA.

On one of my visits, I realized it was Guru Poornima. I decided to visit my old school. I met Mary teacher, another pivotal figure in my life. She was, however, no longer a teacher. She was now the headmistress of the school. The school had the basic infrastructure of a ground floor and a floor above it. Mary ma'am was happy to see me. She took me on a tour of the premises. As we were walking around, I saw a boy drinking water from the toilet tap. I was shocked. I turned to her and asked why the conditions were so dire. She admonished me by saying that it was easy to find faults. The school ran on grants, and the people who previously funded the school were still financing it.

They were doing their best, but they were not really affluent enough to do better. I then called some of my former classmates who were now working as engineers and architects. We got together and funded a water-filtration plant for the school. The tank was installed on the roof of the school building. It provided 25 taps for filtered water along the school corridor. We wanted to give back to our alma mater, and we were proud of what we did.

However, I was humbled when I retook the tour of the school with Mary ma'am. We met a boy named Akash. I was introduced to the boy as one of the people who had facilitated the availability of filtered drinking water in the school. The boy thanked me and then looked me in the eye and asked if I could fulfill one request. I smiled and nodded.

The boy then asked, "Uncle! Can I fill one bottle of water and take it home? I want my parents to drink this pure filtered water as well." With tears in my eyes, I told him to take as much as he wanted. Today, we have established an alumni association that is 1000 members strong. We work to uplift the school and its stakeholders. This association is not just about cutting checks. We organize medical camps, book camps, etc. A boy and a teacher taught me that the world was so much more than what I had thought and perceived it to be. At this juncture, it would be ideal to look at the etymology of the word empathy. The word has two Greek root words. One is pathos, which means feeling.

The other word is em, which means in. So, empathy is about in-feeling. So, when you look at someone, you look at their life from their viewpoint. I came to understand and appreciate this at a dinner event. I was once invited to a cocktail dinner at Sudhir Shenoy's house. Sudhir was the ex-CEO of Dow Chemicals. He had invited a person by the name of Divyanshu Ganatra as a guest for dinner. Divyanshu was the founder of a group called Adventures Beyond Barriers Foundation (ABBF). He is a pilot, trekker, mountaineer, scuba diver, and marathoner. Impressed? What if I also tell you that he is visually impaired?

He is India's first solo blind pilot and the first blind pillion cyclist to ride from Manali to Khardung La. Sudhir had invited a group of us to interact with Divyanshu. We were milling around the hall, and we were talking to one another. Most of us knew each other, and we were catching up on the news of our families. We treated ourselves to a few appetizers.

Soon, Divyanshu joined us, and many of us talked to him for a few minutes. As we kept talking, there was a common theme to our questions. We all wanted to know how we could interact with people like Divyanshu better. At this point, one of the servers came by and offered us glasses of wine. Divyanshu picked up a goblet, and using a fork lying on a tray nearby, tapped the goblet bowl. The glass chime made all of us look toward him. He smiled and said, "I always wanted to do this."

We all smiled, and then he asked for a few minutes of our time. "I get this question a lot. They may come in different forms, but however, it is about my disability." He air-quoted when he said disability. He then asked us, "How many of you need reading glasses or spectacles to read your reports?" Many of us, including me, raised our hands. He then turned to Sudhir and asked, "Sudhirji, do you have some newspapers and magazines?" We all were surprised by this question. We were not sure why he wanted them. Sudhir answered in the affirmative and brought a bunch of magazines and newspapers from his study. Divyanshu then asked him to give one each to the people who had raised their hands.

He then said, "Friends, I want you to remove your glasses and try to read whatever you have in your hand." We all removed our visual aids and tried to read. Some of us could read haltingly. I, unfortunately, could not make out the words clearly. The font size was a little too small for clarity. He then asked us a pertinent question, "Do you think of yourself as being disabled?" When we answered, "No," he again asked us, "You cannot see clearly without an external aid. How are we different? You have your glasses; I have my cane. So, what gives people the right to call me disabled?" That conversation changed my perspective. He did not want pity from us. He wanted to be treated the same as we would treat any 'normal' person.

He wanted us to empathize with him and not pity him. What is the difference? Pity comes with the context of condescension and a position of superiority. Empathy allows you to walk in another's shoes. It asks you to look at the world through their eyes. When you look at the world from the viewpoint of others, you keep your ego in check. You will realize that you are not at the center of the world. I found this out personally when I ran my first marathon at the age of 53. However, I was running with a visually impaired person, Ajay. I was his running guide. I had to ensure that he never stumbled or tripped during the whole event. As I ran the entire marathon, I personally witnessed the courage and perseverance of Ajay. Every pothole or break in the asphalt felt different. But he ran all the same. It happens to be one of the most fulfilling experiences of my life.

If you are in a leadership position, you may think that empathy might hamper you. I knew an office boy named Nilesh. I interacted with him regularly. I did not place any importance on the stations we held or the office hierarchy. Unfortunately, the COVID pandemic claimed his life. I called his home to convey my condolences. His wife answered the call and thanked me. She told me that her husband had talked a lot about me. She told me that I knew more about him and his family than many of his friends. You will come to realize that empathy is never about entitlement. It never belittles you. Instead, empathy endears you to others.

Everyone has a desire to be heard and understood. When we are misunderstood, we ail greatly. But when we have empathy, it helps us reach within us and get in touch with our emotions. We understand ourselves better and ask ourselves to understand others better as well. As I said earlier, values are what make us human beings. One can be cunning or sly, but there are enough fables that teach us how these traits can never aid in the long term. If you were to look at those fables, you would see that animals are generally used as examples to depict these negative values. Remember the sly snake or the cunning jackal? But when you think of qualities like honesty, integrity, or empathy, you think of people like Mahatma Gandhi, Abraham Lincoln, Nelson Mandela, Martin Luther King Jr, etc. These people are considered as paragons of humanity.

What kind of values do you want to be known for—human values or those lacking humanity?

"The value of life is not in its duration but in its donation. You are not important because of how long you live, you are important because of how effective you live."
—Myles Munroe

4

VALUES

"Keep your thoughts positive because your thoughts become your words. Keep your words positive because your words become your behaviour. Keep your behaviour positive because your behaviour becomes your habits. Keep your habits positive because your habits become your values. Keep your values positive because your values become your destiny."
— Mahatma Gandhi

I can almost hear the groans from the cynics among you. You must be wondering why you should read a chapter that stresses the importance of values. You may even contend that you have learned this from your childhood. But, worry not. I am not here to judge you or your values. This is not a book on morals. For example, some radicals may suggest that consumption of non-vegetarian fare is immoral. However, I hold no such judgment. Unless you have deep personal religious beliefs, assigning any sort of moral quality to daily habits is pointless. What I want to explore here is the importance of reflecting on yourself and your values. You need to test the strength of these values and your faith in them. If you can pardon me for being slightly instructional here, I just have one thing to emphasize: Never lose your morals. I am reminded of a story at this point. Several years ago, there was a soldier who always wore his regimental tie and lapel pin wherever he went.

Even when people stared at him with judgment, he wore it unfailingly. He was in the habit of riding on the bus from his house to the city's downtown area. He used to provide the exact fare for these rides. However, on one occasion, he did not have the exact fare. He gave the bus driver a larger denomination of currency and received the balance. When he seated himself, he noticed that he had been given an extra quarter. He was now perplexed. He thought to himself, "Should I keep it? No, it is not the right thing to do. I have to give it back." Then as if the devil whispered to him, another thought intruded, "It is only a quarter. I am sure the driver would not have noticed. Anyway, he sees many people, and I am sure he will not miss such a minuscule amount of money. No one will know. I shall take it as a gift from God."

However, when he reached his destination, he hesitated. He turned from the exit door and extended his hand to the driver. It had the extra quarter. He told the driver, "I think you gave me an extra quarter." The driver smiled. He replied, "I have noticed you wear your army credentials proudly. My son has been wanting to join the army. I have heard of how it instills character in young men, and I wanted to ask a soldier about the process to become one. However, when I saw you, I wanted to test the idea that army men are principled. I wanted to see what you would do if I gave you an extra quarter. You passed the test with flying colors. You have been principled even over an extra quarter. Can you please tell me how my son can become a soldier like you?"

When the soldier stepped off the bus, he said a silent prayer, "Oh God, I almost sold you and my beloved army out for a mere quarter." So, it is vital that you stick to your principles and never stray away from them. You may find yourself in a position like that soldier who was tested over merely a quarter. You will never know who is watching! However, just like in the soldier's case, when you think that nobody is watching, there will always be one witness.

"Your core values are the deeply held beliefs that authentically describe your soul." – John C. Maxwell

Let us take this quote from Michael Jordan: "*I've missed more than 9000 shots in my career. I've lost almost 300 games. 26 times, I've been trusted to take the game-winning shot and missed. I've failed over and over and over again in my life. And that is why I succeed*" Michael Jordan will go down in history as one of the greatest, if not the greatest, players to have played the game of basketball.

Eagle-eyed coaches and business leaders frequently use this quote to inspire their charges. They stress how even the great Michael Jordan failed on occasions. There can be chest-thumping speeches that can use this quote to talk about the need for perseverance and the relentless need to keep chasing success even when you fail.

If you have watched the documentary, *The Last Dance*, you would have seen that fierce competitive spirit in Jordan. However, when you look back on this quote, you will see something else shine through. It was his integrity toward the game. He did not want to miss a game, even when injured. One of Jordan's teammates, the celebrated Scottie Pippen, once had to leave a game midway because he was sick.

Needless to say, Jordan did not take a kindly view to this. He never missed practice. He ensured that there was an avenue for practice even when he was making the Space Jam movie. His integrity to his craft meant that he was the leader of the pack. When his wayward teammate Dennis Rodman went absent without permission and missed a few games, Jordan turned up at his hotel room and ensured he was back in the game. Sure, Jordan was competitive; there are many stories to prove it.

However, behind that fire was his integrity toward his game. He practiced hard to maintain his level of competence, if not surpass it. Positive values help ground our personality. They are essential in our quest to grow and develop. They play a fundamental part in shaping the future we aspire to create and share. Think of any organization or even an individual. It could also be you. Examine a typical day in the life of your subject. In your case, there could have been many decisions you might have taken today; maybe it is the choice to read this book!

If you are thinking of an organization, there will be lot more decisions involved, and some of them may be of greater gravity in monetary terms. But all these decisions made in a day are the reflection of the values of either the individual or the organization.

There is always a purpose behind these decisions. The purpose is to satisfy individual or organizational needs. How does that work? Let us take the example of a car. A car needs an engine system and a steering system to move and reach a destination. The mission and purpose are like the engine in an organization, and the values are its steering system. This is why organizations have a mission statement and a vision statement. The vision statement outlines the goal, but the mission statement outlines and quantifies how we reach that goal. When values dictate our decisions, we define what is important. It is not just about the 'what' but also the 'how' of a plan. When we draw such clear lines and are able to share them with those around us, we are not just building camaraderie but cohesion as well.

But 'values' is such a broad term. There can be many things that fall under its purview. Let us examine them from the broadest sense to the individual view. The first type of values is societal values. These values show how you or your organization relate to the wider society. Some examples could be sustainability, environmental awareness, planning for the future instead of short-term gains, etc. People can sometimes ignore the small part they can play in the betterment of our society. It is easy to despair about how the rest of the world does not do it, and it may be hard to maintain the same fire with time. Have you heard of the story of starfishes strewn across a beach?

The story goes that one day a colossal wave deposited a lot of starfishes on a beach. This beach was not frequented by either the tourists or the locals. However, on this particular day, a man had come to the beach. The entire beach was filled with starfishes. As far as he could see, the whole coast was blanketed by the starfishes. It was then he saw that he was not alone. He saw another man going around the beach, and noticed how he picked up one starfish and threw it into the ocean.

He smiled at the generosity of the man as he continued to throw the starfishes into the ocean one by one. However, he expected him to stop soon. But the man continued picking up the starfishes and throwing them back into the ocean. When this went on for a while, the man approached him and said, "Sir! Why are you throwing the fish back into the ocean? There is nobody else nearby, and you will barely make a difference. There are so many on the beach. Why do you toil so?"

The other man paused, picked up another starfish, and then turned toward his questioner. He said, "It makes a difference to this starfish."

The second type of values is organizational values. The name is indicative. These are the values that reflect what you and your organization are about. Teamwork, alliances, productivity, etc., are examples of this type. If you follow any Western media, you would have heard of the news of advertisers boycotting some programs because of the content they air. They avoid such programs because they feel that their values do not mesh with those depicted in the program.

Next, we have the relationship values. They include care, generosity, openness, and trust. How trustworthy are you in your relationships? There is the tale of a builder. The builder was one of the savviest players in the game. He knew where to cut corners without getting caught. He greased the right palms during inspections and was able to get rich quickly. He also had ready excuses whenever he received a complaint. He also had the gift of the gab. He knew how to charm people and get out of sticky situations. Then he fell in love with a girl. The girl, too, liked him. They had also discussed about getting married, and were planning to meet their respective parents. It was at this juncture that a big contract landed on his table.

A wealthy man had given him a massive plot of land and asked him to build a house. He was given complete carte-blanche on the planning and execution. The wealthy man simply said, "Build me the best house you can. Money is not of importance.

Think of it as your masterpiece." However, the builder focused only on the second statement. He knew that this man could be fleeced. This became even more evident when he never showed up for any meetings and simply trusted the builder to do a good job. The builder inflated the prices and made a considerable profit. He used sub-standard materials where he could do so without getting caught. Even as he did so, he had a few reservations. The plot of land was identical to the one where he wanted to build a dream house for himself and his wife. Soon he had the house ready. He then invited the client to see the house. It looked glamorous from the outside.

But the builder knew it was not as robust as it looked. When he gave the key to the older man, he received a huge smile in return. The old man pressed the key back into his hand and said, "My daughter has told me a lot about you. She told me that she wants to marry you. So, I wanted you to build a dream house for both of you. Take the key, and I hope you lead a great life here. This house is my wedding present to you." The final type of values is individual values. They reflect you and the principles with which you live your life. Enthusiasm, humility, adaptability, and integrity are all examples of personal values. I have already stressed the importance of integrity. There is another famous story of a baker and cowherd. The cowherd sold all kinds of dairy products. The baker needed butter on a daily basis for his products. He approached the cowherd to work out a deal.

They agreed that they would barter three kilograms of bread and butter every week. The bread would be part of the weekly diet of the cowherd. In return, he only needed to provide three kilograms of butter to the baker. This barter went on for months. One day the baker noticed that the butter delivered did not weigh three kilograms. He assumed it as an innocent oversight and let it go. However, he soon noticed that the quantity of butter was slowly decreasing. He was enraged and approached the cowherd. The cowherd, however, protested his innocence. The baker had no choice but to drag him to a judge to help mediate the matter.

The judge heard the complaint and then asked the cowherd, "You have heard the complaint. Do you accept the charge?" The cowherd again vehemently stressed his innocence. The judge then asked the butter to be weighed. It was less than three kilograms. The cowherd was shocked. He said, "That is not possible. I check it every time." The judge then asked if his weights could be brought to the court as they could be faulty. The cowherd replied that he did not have any weights. Then the judge asked, "If you do not have any weights, how did you weigh out three kilograms?" The cowherd answered, "I used the bread given by the baker as my measure." The previous two stories are the perfect illustration of how compromising on your values will ultimately affect you the most.

"Values are like fingerprints. Nobodies are the same, but you leave them all over everything you do."
– Elvis Presley

From an organizational perspective, values are critical in fostering and maintaining a harmonious work culture. They outline how the employees should work. They provide the guidelines as to how any activity is to be performed. These guidelines form part of the orientation programs conducted by organizations for their new employees.

Values set the range of acceptable behaviors for the employees and the leader alike. It makes clear the actions that are recommended and encouraged and the actions that can be detrimental. These guidelines help people make decisions unhesitatingly and with greater precision.

They also determine hiring processes and performance evaluations. When values are not placed at the center of decision making, you will see the kind of fallout that occurred after the 2008 financial crisis. Financial institutions placed importance on the financial prudence of the people they had loaned money to. But in the build-up to the 2008 crisis, they gave out loans with outrageous interest rates without any care.

There was a lot of money to be made from subprime loans, and everyone wanted a share of the pie. They compromised on the values as they thought that the American mortgage market was infallible. If we learn anything from that crisis, it is to never depend on external factors to bail us out. Only our values can provide a safe harbor from the fiercest storms.

"Our value is the sum of our values." – Joe Batten

An organization may outline its values. But you as an individual must be able to align with the same values. Most people who suffer from workplace fatigue and burnout are the people who are not able to align their values with those of the company. For example, if a person stays at a job just for the high salary package, he/she will be able to work but not as efficiently or effectively.

Look at any great entrepreneurial story. People quit cushy jobs to take risks to chase their passion. Their values of adventure and courage did not mesh with the safe and conservative values of the company they worked for.

Values in Leadership

Leadership values are essential as they will determine what kind of leader you will be. It will set the roadmap on how you wish to achieve your goals. These values will not just be important for your professional enhancement; they will also be vital in your personal development. When you possess a strong set of core values, it will help in building credibility and trust among your team members. These values of leadership are crucial for the success of each individual:

- Adventurousness
- Authenticity
- Commitment
- Compassion

- Concern for others
- Consistency
- Courage
- Dependability

When you are at your workplace, ask yourself a few questions. These will help you consider your values and your organization's values. The first question would be to inquire whether your personal values align with that of the organization. The second question should be to observe if your current work and decisions related to it are driven by a combination of all the four values we discussed above. If they are not, ask yourself why is it not? Where are you falling short? The next question is essential, especially when you hold a leadership position. Are the values of the organization followed at the workplace?

If your answer is yes, find out how it benefits the work culture and environment. If the answer is no, find out where it is needed and how it can be adopted.

"I never wanted to be on any billionaires list. I never define myself by net worth. I always try to define myself by my values."
– Howard Schultz.

5

SOAR THE SKIES, REMEMBER THE ROOTS

"True humility is intelligent self-respect which keeps us from thinking too highly or too meanly of ourselves. It makes us modest by reminding us how far we have come short of what we can be."
— Ralph W. Sockman

The year was 2009. I was still in the USA. I had seen the country elect Barack Obama as the President of the United States of America in 2008. It was the first year of his presidency. It was around October that I received an invitation to the White House.

Manmohan Singh, the then Prime Minister of India, was coming over for a state visit. His visit coincided with the festival of Diwali. Hence, the First Lady, Michelle Obama, had decided to host Manmohan Singh and his delegation at the White House with a welcome tea party.

Manmohan Singh's delegation included many business magnates and leaders from India. So, Michelle Obama had sent out invitations to many business leaders and executive-level employees of leading businesses in the country. Those of us who had Indian roots were preferred.

I held a senior position as President of a non-profit community organization, India Forum Inc., and received invitations for my wife and me. When I showed the invitation, my wife was excited as well. The date was set for 25th November. Fortunately, I had a relatively free day. I intimated to my secretary to reschedule my appointments for that day and to keep it free. I also immediately confirmed with the organizers that my wife, Jyothi and I would be attending the event. That day was very memorable and the memories remain vivid even now. We met with many people, and we were able to interact with many of the NRIs present at the event. I also met some business partners, and it was a fabulous party hosted inside the White House. We were served good tea and Indian snacks. As we were mingling in the busy event, my wife spied a notable figure in the distance.

She nudged me and pointed to a small crowd. I could see that people were crowding around one person. I could only see his back. He seemed to be wearing an immaculate suit and had grey hair. He was quite tall and seemed larger than life. Even though his hair hinted at an older age, his bearing seemed to suggest otherwise. He seemed to be energetic and was making his audience laugh as he told them a few jokes.

Suddenly, he turned around, and I could see why my wife was excited to see him. She turned to me and said, "Satish! Let us go and say hello." While I wanted to meet him, I decided to hint otherwise to my wife. Playfully, I told her, "He is Ratan Tata. He must be very busy. Anyway, why do you want to meet him?" She replied, "You do know that my first job was at TELCO. It is a Tata company. I have to meet him and also thank him for the opportunity." I joked, "Well! He did not personally give you the job." However, we did walk toward him.

When we reached him, I extended my hand to introduce myself. He smiled broadly and extended his hand as well. I introduced myself and gave him my business card. Then I introduced my wife and told him that she had started her career at TELCO. His smile grew even broader, and he enquired about our health and how we came to be in America. He then noticed my business card.

It said that I worked at McCormick. When he saw the name, he put his hand on my shoulder and said, "Young man! Please convey my regards to the McCormick family." I was surprised but said that I would do so. As far as I knew, McCormick had no business dealings with Tata. Even as we talked further, this thought continued to plague me. I did not ask him why he wanted me to convey his regards.

Soon, we drifted away and went in different directions. My wife was also curious as to why he wanted his regards to be conveyed to the McCormick family. The tea party continued on with good music and good cheer. Soon Mr. Manmohan Singh and his delegation prepared to leave the White House, marking the end of the evening's festivities. They were departing in a single file. My wife and I watched the line inch its way out the door.

Then we saw Ratan Tata once again. Coincidentally, he too saw us at the same time. He broke rank from the line and walked toward us. He once again put his arms around my shoulders and said, "Young man! Please do ensure that you convey my warmest regards to the McCormick family." I nodded and assured him that I would definitely convey his regards and his message.

I was genuinely surprised by his insistence that I convey his regards. Even as I slept that night, I could not help but wonder why. The next day, I went to the office and tried to look up in the company files if McCormick ever had any dealings with Tata. I could not find the record of any such dealings. I enquired of a few trusted people, but none of them had a clue either. I had to set my curiosity aside for the moment. I drafted an e-mail detailing the fact that Mr. Ratan Tata, one of India's leading industrialists, wanted to convey his warm regards to the McCormick family.

I conveyed his message, and I also politely tried to enquire about his relationship with McCormick. I sent the e-mail to the McCormick leadership. I received an e-mail acknowledging my mail and also thanking me for conveying his message. I did not receive any input regarding Ratan Tata's relationship with the McCormick family.

Soon, I heard on the company grapevine that Mr. Tata used to be a guest at one of the McCormick homes when he used to study at Boston, 40 years ago. Generally, he used to stay for a few days during the holidays. That was the only connection I could find.

However, I had to shed my detective hat as I had other pressing matters to attend to. I put this in the back of my mind and forgot all about it. A few years later, I decided to return to my earlier site of 'failure', India. I wanted to plant the flag of the world's biggest spice company in the biggest spice market in the world. (I shall cover this in a later chapter) As part of these efforts, I got the chance to visit a potential company which we hoped to acquire.

The President of McCormick was also joining me on this trip. I suddenly remembered my conversation with Ratan Tata. The company we were interested in was based in Mumbai, and I knew that there was the possibility of arranging a meeting with Mr. Ratan Tata. Accordingly, I drafted an e-mail to him introducing myself as Satish Rao, a senior executive at McCormick. I mentioned our meeting at the White House in 2009. I told him that the President of McCormick and I were coming to India on a business trip. I asked if we could have the pleasure of meeting him in Mumbai while we there. Being slightly presumptuous, I informed him of the dates we were free during the trip.

His reply was prompt. He said that he did remember me. He also added that it would be his pleasure to host us and picked a date from the list I had sent him. I immediately messaged the President that we could have a personal appointment with Ratan Tata. He, too, was happy with the date and conveyed his pleasure in meeting him. I quickly replied to Mr. Tata's mail and told him that it would be our privilege and honor to be hosted by him.

The appointment was fixed for evening tea at Bombay House, the corporate headquarters of the Tata group. I made the trip to Mumbai to start the process for a possible entry into the Indian market. It was an exciting time; however, I was equally excited to meet Mr. Tata. On the allotted day, we had a long morning session with the management of the potential acquisition. It was a tiring day.

However, as we took the car ride to Bombay House, I could feel my energy return. When we reached Bombay House, we were immediately taken by the architecture of the building. I was as giddy as I had been on my first day at Bayer. I had the same nervous energy, and I could not help but feel awed at what was about to happen. We were immediately treated as VIPs.

We were ushered into a lovely waiting room. It was stately and impressive. When we seated ourselves on the sofas, it seemed like we had sunk into cushion heaven. It was the perfect antidote to a long tiring day of business negotiations. I turned to one of the people in the room and asked him when we could expect Mr. Tata. Suddenly, I heard a voice from the side of the room. There was a staircase there down which came Mr. Tata. He was carefully walking down and was holding a tray. I immediately sprang up to go and help him. He said, "Please be seated, young man. You are the guest in my home. It is my duty to be the host." He then personally set the tray onto the table and served us tea. He did not ask for help from any other person. We then went on to have a wonderful conversation. It was in the midst of that conversation that I remembered my curiosity. I could not help myself but ask, "Sir, I had conveyed your message and regards to the McCormick family. However, I was curious as to how you knew them. As far as I looked and enquired, McCormick has never had any kind of business dealings with Tata." He smiled and said, "Young man! We may not have had any business dealings with them. I, however, am indebted to them. When I studied in Boston, they welcomed me with open arms. They were generous and hospitable. They took care of me when I was there, especially during the times I stayed over in the holidays. Those were some memorable days. I will always be grateful to them for opening their doors and welcoming me into their home. However, with time, we drifted away from each other. Life took us in different directions. But when you produced that card, I knew I had to reconnect. So, I asked you to convey my regards." I was surprised by his emotions. Soon, the conversation moved to other topics, and we had a wonderful time together.

However, the time was too short, and we had to leave. He was gracious and humorous. If you were to remove his labels or the grandeur of Bombay House, you would have looked at that scene and thought of a kind, warm man who was bidding farewell to a couple of old friends. He came with us till the gate. He opened the car door for both the President and me. He was insistent that he was the host and that he had to bid us goodbye.

I was extremely humbled by his behavior. Here was a man who had seen it all and done it all and was one of the leading businessmen in the world. However, he did not find anything demeaning in serving tea to his guests or opening the car doors for them as a courtesy when they were leaving. Shetty Teacher's words of educating myself rang through my head. Here was a man who had inherited wealth. He possessed a last name that will hold currency in any part of the world. But here he was reminiscing about his good memories and being grateful. He had reached such heights, yet he was so humble.

Humility is one of the most important attributes one needs to cultivate. It gives one the perspective needed. One will place greater respect on one's place in the world. It is about accepting one's weakness and appreciating the thoughts, actions, and perspectives of others. To be truly humble, one needs self-awareness, self-esteem, and self-control. This means that a humble leader will be open to input and advice from others.

Humble leaders will never display arrogance that they have all the solutions needed. They will involve everyone in their team to produce the best effort, and, consequently, the best result. When a leader loses humility, they do not place any importance on their staff. They lose the traits of compassion and empathy as well because all their intentions and actions will be driven by self-interest. When their deeds are driven by self-interest, they will also close their minds for any valuable feedback or constructive criticism. When the team serves the interest of the leader, the leader will then lose the respect and admiration of the team members. When you are humble, it shows that you are always looking to learn.

Nelson Mandela once said, "...*the first thing is, to be honest with yourself. You can never have an impact on society if you have not changed yourself...Great peacemakers are all people of integrity, of honesty, ... humility.*"

Humility is a virtue that is highly discounted these days. Look at any popular culture or media; heroes are put on a pedestal. The rise of influencers in social media has also seen the rise of the 'me-culture.' People look to external validation with ostentatious displays of personal worth. Modern music lyrics celebrate fame, money, and self-aggrandizement.

There is a hunger for social media likes and comments, and these standards set the mood for the day. The pursuit of excellence has now been reduced to the pursuit of applause for that excellence. It is easy to get trapped in this pursuit and to follow the latest trend. The modern lifestyle is all about praise—self-praise as well as praise from others. It is easy to fall into such fruitless pursuits. Humility will prevent you from falling into these traps.

Humility is grounded in confidence. Humility is not about bowing your head. It is about looking the goal square in the eye. It is what keeps you focused even as loud cheers accompany you on the side. It is easy to get tempted and distracted by the commendations you receive. Humility, as Sockman said, lets us know that there is still a way to go. Humility is an essential trait for concentration. Humble people are confident in their strengths. They know that they have a plan to accomplish their goals, and they are confident in their ability to execute it. Their humility lets them soar, but reminds them that they have to return to the ground to soar once more. When you lose your humility, you tend to become overconfident. Overconfidence leads to complacency. There is a reason that one of the moral stories taught to children carries the adage: Pride comes before a fall.

There can be a misconception that humility means subservience. It is not so. Humility is about respect and dignity. It shines a light on your flaws and the areas you need to improve. It allows you to see the value of others and how they can help you do better. I am sure you have seen the CRED ad with Rahul Dravid.

It shows him as an angry man in a volatile traffic jam and hilariously ends with Dravid declaring himself as the *gunda* of Indiranagar. It became a viral sensation. CRED made other adverts with other equally or more famous people. But why did Dravid's advert gain such traction? It was because we have never seen him in that avatar. Rahul Dravid was part of a generation of masterful batsmen. Even in such great company, Dravid made a mark for himself. When he had flamboyant characters with him, Dravid let his bat do the talking. He was humble in the face of praise and gracious when defeated.

So, when the advert showed him as a man just like the rest of us, it became a huge hit. It was this juxtaposition of his acting with his real nature that made the advertisement a viral sensation. Humility is also about accepting when you are wrong. The greatest caricatures and falls are subjected to those who have too much pride. The most horrible bosses are not those who assign challenging tasks, but those who are quick to take the praise and quicker in passing the blame. Humility is about doing the right thing. Football Leaks was a platform that revealed financial scandals that implicated many clubs and players for corrupt practices. When N'Golo Kante's name was included in a Football Leaks report, people were stunned. Kante, the all-action midfielder, is one of those beloved players who was not trapped by the tribalism generally invoked by the game.

However, people looked into the matter closely, and Football Leaks said Kante was as squeaky-clean as his image suggested. Many players have been paid their salaries via an offshore company. As per a report in Media Part, Kante did establish an offshore company in a tax haven as per the request of his club, Chelsea. However, he changed his mind and wanted to be paid normally. His agent would tell the club that Kante was inflexible and that he wanted a normal salary.

Kante's humility was seen in his behavior. When his teammates turned up in the latest supercars and hypercars, he drove around in a Mini Cooper. It was the first car he had bought, and he liked it. So even when he gained great riches, he continued driving his old car.

Kante was never a teenage prodigy. He only made his professional debut at the age of 21, unlike some of his gifted compatriots. Kante would move to Leicester at the age of 23 and would win the fairytale EPL title at the age of 24. He would move to Chelsea the following year and win it again. In the six years since winning the EPL title with Leicester, he would win all the major club titles available in England and also a World Cup with France in 2018. He would play crucial roles in all those triumphs in the midfield. However, even with all his major honors, Kante remains the same humble person.

If you were to look up Kante, you would find many such stories like accepting a fan's dinner invitation, among others. His humility has endeared him to the football audience at large and seen him avoid the trappings of any form of football tribalism.

Humility is about understanding our place in the larger scheme of things. There is a story of a man who was out riding a horse when he saw a few soldiers struggling to move a heavy log of wood. Their struggles were to no avail as they were not able to move it. He saw another man looking on at the futile efforts of the soldiers. He could not hold back his curiosity. He was shocked that the man was not lending a hand. He went up to him and asked why he was not helping those soldiers. The man replied that he was the corporal. He added further that he gave orders, and he expected the soldiers to follow them. It was not within his remit to help them move that log. The reply silenced the horse rider. He did not retort; instead, he dismounted, and under the watchful eyes of the corporal, he went ahead and helped the soldiers in heaving the log of wood. This time, the soldiers were able to move it with the help of the additional man. He then mounted the horse and said to the corporal that he should send for the Commander-in-Chief the next time his men needed help. The horse rider was none other than George Washington.

Stories of humility never make the press. News is about personalities, and the world today is about narcissism. Narcissistic displays could make you stand out, but it is humility that secures your spot. There is a phrase: fifteen minutes of fame.

This phrase is especially relevant today in the age of social media stars and influencers. Their images and videos might show them living the grand life of opulence and luxury. However, if you look into it deeper, you will find stories of depression, drug abuse, and other related issues due to the need to maintain the façade. You may stand out with narcissistic displays, but you will never inspire a sense of reliability and confidence with such an attitude. People may dismiss you as a show-off. But when you are humble, you will be regarded as the bulwark of your team. People will know that they can rely on you and hold you in high regard. I came from the chawl.

Even today, as a CEO, I have not forgotten my roots. I have made friends and acquaintances at high places. But my bosom friends are the ones I made in my childhood. The friendships made during childhood are pure and without any reciprocal intent. There is no quid-pro-quo nature attached to these relationships. You become friends because you want to be friends and not because you see some potential benefits. When I was living abroad for two decades, whenever I returned to India during the holidays, I made it a point to meet up with my old friends at least once. I have continued that habit to this day. We meet every month, and we eat out in the local eateries. We engage in some good-natured ribbing between us. I have eaten at the most palatial of hotels, but the joy I get in sharing Vada Pav at the local stall with my friends is unparalleled. These friends know the real Satish Rao, devoid of any labels. They befriended me because I am Satish Rao, the boy who grew up with them. They did not befriend me because I am Satish Rao, the CEO. People may have varied thoughts about our friendships. But I learn from them every day. I can see it in the integrity and honesty they show in their work and relationships. They remind me of the lessons I learned from my childhood.

"Have more humility. Remember, you don't know the limits of your own abilities. Successful or not, if you keep pushing beyond yourself, you will enrich your own life--and maybe even please a few strangers."
- A.L. Kennedy

In many years, I have seen the many benefits of humility. People will value their time with you. They will genuinely seek your company and enjoy it. They will understand that you too value them. They will feel the dignity and respect you give them. Secondly, humility will help you identify your faults. It will shine a light on where the gaps in your knowledge are so that you bridge them.

There is nothing to be gained from a show of bravado. It is like the adage, "*The man who asks a question is a fool for a minute, the man who does not ask is a fool for life.*"

Humility is about the acceptance of being the fool in the pursuit of knowledge and excellence. You will keep learning as you will know that you are not all-knowing. You will have a childlike thirst for knowledge. When you are truly humble, you will never think that admitting your ignorance is a sign of weakness or an embarrassment.

No one is immune to criticism. As humans, we can never be perfect. So, we are bound to make mistakes. But humility will never allow you to dwell on them for too long. It is only when you think of yourself as infallible that a trip would seem like an almighty fall. When you are humble, you will be able to dust yourself off and carry on after learning from the mistake.

Think of the most influential people in your life. My parents played such a pivotal role in my life because they were patient with me. The most influential people in your life made that impact in your life because they were patient with you. Humility grants that patience when you deal with others. You will be able to positively impact others' lives when you are patient in your dealings with them.

I leave you with this poem, The Thumb by Amos Russel Wells, which can be considered an ode to humility.

Hail to the thumb, the useful thumb,
The grasper, the holder, the doer of deeds,
Where fingers are futile, and tools succumb,
Stolid, ungainly, the thumb succeeds.
Hail to the thumb, the homely thumb;

Rings and jewels are not for it,
Compliments, dainty and frolicsome,
For fingers are suited, for thumbs unfit
Hail to the thumb, the modest thumb;
Gently and calmly, it hides away,
Never for it a banner and drum,
Or praise at the end of a strenuous day.
And hail to the men who are like the thumb;
Men who are never sung by a bard,
Men who are laboring, modestly dumb,
Faithfully doing the work that is hard
Some day, men of the toiling thumb,
Men of the modest, invincible worth,
Some day your high reward will come
From the Hand of the Lord of heaven and earth!

6

HUMILITY

"Humility is the foundation of all the other virtues hence, in the soul in which this virtue does not exist there cannot be any other virtue except in mere appearance."
—Saint Augustine

I am sure that all of you have heard of Aesop's Fables. You may have also heard of the Parables, Panchatantra Tales, etc. They all are short stories that provide us with a great moral lesson at the end. I want to relate a Buddhist fable. Buddhism, like every religion, asks its practitioners to meditate on God with the help of chants, psalms, and mantras. This is the story of a Buddhist monk. He was a very proud monk. He lived in a monastery, where he meditated on a mantra for several years.

He sought guidance from the many senior monks present within the monastery. It was said that he meditated on a particular mantra with great focus. His efforts led him to attain great insights. He then took up teaching the mantra to the devotees. However, he no longer looked to his senior monks for guidance.

He felt that they no longer had anything to teach him. He felt like he was the top expert on this particular mantra. It was at this juncture that he learned of a reclusive monk, a hermit. The reclusive monk lived on a small island in the middle of the lake.

The enterprising monk felt that this was an opportunity he could not miss. He thought he could perhaps learn something more from this hermit that his senior brothers could not impart to him at the monastery. With this aim, he enlisted the help of a local boatman to ferry him across the lake. He then met the hermit on the island. The hermit welcomed him and brewed him some tea. As they were partaking of the tea, the younger monk asked him about his spiritual practice. The hermit contritely remarked that he had no spiritual practice. He only meditated on a particular mantra. When the younger monk enquired further, he was pleasantly shocked that the hermit meditated on the same mantra. He felt like this was meant to be. He then asked the hermit for guidance. But he was soon horrified.

He heard the hermit recite the mantra and he was shocked to hear him mispronounce it. The hermit saw the shock displayed on his guest's face. He asked him if anything was wrong. The younger monk told him that his pronunciation was incorrect. The hermit, too, was shocked. He immediately asked the younger monk to help him rectify his mistake. The younger monk then immediately chanted out the correct pronunciation of the mantra. The hermit thanked him and asked if he could be excused as he wanted to meditate on it without delay. The younger monk nodded and embarked on the boat to make his return journey.

He could not help but sigh on the boat. He thought to himself, "It is unfortunate that he practiced it incorrectly for so long. By Buddha's grace, I met him at least before he is on his deathbed and corrected him. Even if his time in this world is short, he will be meditating correctly." He then realized that the boat was not moving. He looked at his boatman, only to see his mouth agape at a sight behind his back. He turned to see the hermit standing on the water. He looked at the monk respectfully. The hermit first apologized. He apologized for inconveniencing the monk as he had forgotten the correct pronunciation. He wanted him to repeat the correct pronunciation so that he could learn it again. Our proud monk was awestruck.

He stuttered and replied that the hermit did not need a mantra. However, the hermit politely persisted. The monk had no choice but to repeat the mantra. The hermit listened carefully and went through every syllable as if imprinting it into his memory. He then thanked the monk, repeated the mantra, and walked across the lake's surface back to the island.

You do not need me to tell you the significance of the story. Perhaps you will find the lesson in how pride can affect even monks and how you should actively look to avoid this particular vice. However, the more incredible lesson comes from the hermit. Even when he had reached such significant heights in his spiritual sojourn, he was willing to learn humbly from a monk about the correct pronunciation of a mantra he had meditated on.

"Humility is the true key to success. Successful people lose their way at times. They often embrace and overindulge from the fruits of success. Humility halts this arrogance and self-indulging trap. Humble people share the credit and wealth, remaining focused and hungry to continue the journey of success."
– Rick Pitino.

We could all do with a little bit of humility. Let us look at our films. Be it regional movies or the Bollywood ones, our heroes are always over sensationalized. 'Mass movies," is a term used in south India for a particular genre of films, and this genre has seen a rapid growth in the number of films produced. The hero is usually portrayed as coming from a humble or poor background, the background score is a crescendo, and there are plenty of one-liner quips made by the hero throughout the movie. All these are accompanied by whistles from the audience when the hero flexes his arms. In all these movies, the emphasis is on the hero's grandstanding and external appearance.

Zlatan Ibrahimović, the Swedish footballer, has been one of the most successful and marketable players in this century. While he never will be ranked in the same tier as Ronaldo and Messi, he will say he is better than them if you were to ask him.

Ibrahimović's ego has brought him many headlines, like reports on how he always refers to himself in the third person. He famously remarked as a teenager that he did not do trials when Arsenal wanted to have a closer look at him before offering a contract.

When asked what gift he would be buying his wife for her birthday, he even famously remarked, "Nothing. She already has Zlatan." He has become a cult figure known for his ego more than his football. But will Zlatan be remembered with the same fondness as Messi is? There is a reason why Pele holds more significant cultural capital in the game of football than Maradona. Their humility endeared them far more to the people than any brash talk of their contemporaries. But humility is challenging. Why? It may be because we have a misconception of the idea. We think of humility as putting ourselves into a corner. We think of it as a sign of weakness.

"Humility is not thinking less of yourself, it's thinking of yourself less."
– Rick Warren

Humility is actually a sign of great inner fortitude and strength. So why is humility necessary? Let us think of it this way. Let us say you meet someone humble. You will find that you can relax in their company. How about we add a little more color to this scenario? Let us say your boss radiates humility. You also know that your boss is demanding, but fair. His humility will remove all stress, and you will find yourself performing far better in this environment. When your boss is humble, you know that your professionalism and talent will endear you to him far more than any brown-nosing will. You must have heard of many horror stories featuring terrible bosses.

Some of these bosses would steal credit from their subordinates and pass the buck when it comes to failures. But when you work for a humble boss, you know you do not have to worry about any of those issues. He/she will stand with you and in front of you during times of distress. You know you will be evaluated only on your work, and you will be accepted for who you are, warts and all.

Would you not like to work in such an environment? You could gift this to your colleagues when you make humility a core part of your personality. People will naturally be attracted to you without knowing why. One of the iconic football managers in the world today is Jurgen Klopp. He does not hold the pedigree of a Pep Guardiola or a Carlo Ancelotti. He did not boast of a playing career worth any repute. But he is charismatic and is one of the most successful managers in the world today. Another managerial great of the game is Jose Mourinho. However, Mourinho's stock in the game has been falling. However, Klopp never faced the same problem despite never having the same list of honors. An examination of their press conferences will provide you with further insight. It is especially visible after a loss. Mourinho will blame the referee, or more commonly, criticize his players for not sticking to the strategy. Klopp, too, deflects by blaming the referee or the pitch, but he would never blame his team. He would instead say that it was his mistake. There is a reason Mourinho's teams self-destruct and are known as three-year projects.

"Humility is not something that comes naturally. But it is a cardinal virtue that should be pursued more than any other."
– Joyce Meyer

Humility means recognizing that you do not know everything. There is a mistaken perception that admitting this can compromise your standing, especially from a leadership standpoint. But, in fact, such an admission will only serve to show your grace and honesty. You bring up your team along with you. Each of your team members will feel like a part of your team rather than a lackey following your orders. Such an admission does not diminish you in any way. Your stature will diminish only when you place more value on Facebook posts and likes, salary packets, and fame. Humility enshrines compassion toward humanity and it helps you become a better person. And in this process of making yourself better, you will make everyone around you better as well.

Cultivating humility is not easy. It does not come on with the turning on of a switch, and it takes time. It takes courage to recognize that you may not be as good as you make out to be. However, when you work toward being humble, you give yourself one of the greatest gifts—freedom to be you. You will no longer be trying to hide facets of yourself that you consider negative. You will permit yourself to be honest with others and, importantly, with yourself. When you are humble, you will be gracious toward yourself and be understanding and compassionate toward others.

Humility and leadership

"A sense of humility is essential to leadership because it authenticates a person's humanity."
– John Baldoni.

Ask any business management expert about humility. They will rank it at the very top of the list of traits needed to be an effective leader. It is the certification of one's humanity. It shows a willingness to learn. I want to reiterate that humility is not putting yourself down; it is merely understanding your strengths and weaknesses and recognizing the strengths of others. How can one lead with humility? Here are three tips:

- Do not be enamored by your position of power. Share it with the people around you. Make them feel welcome and embrace their strengths. Enable them to contribute to the team rather than just being your followers. When you involve them in decision-making, you signal that you trust them and have confidence in their abilities. When they feel that confidence in you, you will build a stronger and more effective team. However, if you micromanage them and ask them to follow every detail that you set without any option for them to contribute, neither you nor your team will ever fulfill the promised potential.

- Be generous when it comes to giving credit. Never be miserly when it comes to acknowledging the efforts of your team. Praise them when they succeed and provide support when they fail. Gratitude is not a sign of weakness; rather, it is a sign of strength. When you make a mistake, do not make excuses. Admit your fault and share your experience. Let them know where you failed so that they do not trip in a similar situation.

Share your learnings and insights. Encourage a culture where people can freely admit their mistakes and are given a chance to do better. If people are scared to admit their mistakes, it will contribute to a toxic work culture. When you build a strict but forgiving culture, it will go a long way in making your team a safe avenue for innovation. If fear is the driving work culture, people will tend to play it safe and not aim for greater heights.

When you provide a culture that encourages people to experiment and innovate, you effectively provide an avenue for people to learn and develop themselves. You do that by allowing them to take responsibilities that ordinary leaders might keep for themselves.

As I mentioned before, humility is one of the most valuable leadership skills. Humble leaders, driven by the desire to learn and grow, are solution-oriented, open-minded, and fair. The humble leader is a mentor, a manager who is not afraid to relinquish control or admit their mistakes.

Here are a few tips for developing humility:

1. Never judge people by your strengths and weaknesses; judge them based on their strengths and weaknesses. You can only obtain success when you understand your team members. Focus on developing their strengths and help them fulfill their potential. Self-reflection should be a daily exercise. I recommend my mirror test.

2. Always temper what you think of yourself with what others think of you. If there is a huge gap between these two positions, it shows that you lack self-awareness. Self-reflection will ensure that you are always self-aware as well.

3. Be thankful when people contribute. Consider their inputs and provide them with consistent feedback. However, I do not mean you should always be looking to provide solace. If a situation demands painful feedback, share that as well.

4. Create environments that nurture and protect excellence. Expect the utmost from yourself.

This brings about the question, "How can I develop humility?" You could embrace what makes you human. Know that we are not perfect. There will be times when you will fall short of expectations, be it others' or your own. This is what makes us human. The problem is that we attach too much importance to these external achievements.

If you find yourself losing, accept it with grace. Then find out where you went wrong, reflect and learn, and move on. But we tend to mope around our failures and regrets. It is easy to fall into the trap of feeling unworthy and loathing yourself. This can be a hard turn from which you might find recovery is not easy. However, when you understand that failures and setbacks are part of the human experience, you will find it easier to shed the oppressive burden of unwanted pressure brought forth by the pursuit of perfection. Another way is to practice self-compassion and mindfulness consciously. It is easy to hate and pity yourself. Once you get used to them, any struggle against such feelings is extremely difficult. Instead, learn to look at yourself without judgment.

"People who are compassionate toward their failings and imperfections experience greater well-being than those who repeatedly judge themselves. The feelings of security and net worth provided by self-compassion are also highly stable, kicking in precisely when self-esteem falls down."
— Kristin Neff.

Lea Seigen Shinraku, a therapist, has an empathetic story of the importance of self-compassion. One Friday at 5 pm, her car broke down on a busy road. Her vehicle had stalled because of the engine overheating. This led to backing up of traffic, and the resounding horns of the vehicles behind her only played as the soundtrack for her self-criticism. She was lamenting the fact that she had not checked her vehicle for all these details earlier.

She called the local towing company and was told that it would take them 30 minutes to arrive. As she sat in her car, berating herself in self-doubt and hate, someone knocked on her car window. She thought it was an irate motorist. But when she brought the window down, the man introduced himself as the owner of the café across the street. He asked her if she needed tea. She felt she was about to break into tears due to the kindness shown by the man, even as he offered her the choice of a chocolate drink or milk, in case she did not like tea. Lea asked for chamomile tea and the man went to get it for her. When she tried to pay for it, he refused to accept. Instead, he simply said, "Hey, I have been there." It was a reminder for her that these things can happen to anyone. Suddenly the man was back and asked her if she was allergic to honey. When she answered in the negative, he replied, "Oh, good. I put honey in it. I did not think to ask if you were allergic. If you are, I can make another one."

This act of kindness breached through her wall of self-criticism. Lea says whenever she finds herself in a similar spot of bother, she would ask herself if she was allergic to honey. It would remind her of that day and stop any thoughts of self-blame. Maybe, you too, have some incident in your life where a random act of kindness from a stranger broke through your self-criticism. Remind yourself of that incident and remember you are a human being, and setbacks happen to everyone.

"Life is a long lesson in humility." – James M. Barrie

7

WHEN THE WORLD WENT WEST, I WENT EAST

"The art of life lies in a constant readjustment to our surroundings."
— Okakura Kakuzō

The date is 24th August, 2004. The 28th modern Olympic Games are currently underway in Athens, Greece. The day is progressing well in Athens and the men's 200 meters heats are ongoing. In the fourth heat, a man on the fifth lane comes fifth in the race. However, his specialty lies in the 200-meter dash. He was not successful in any 200-meter race after the Olympics. This was a blow to the young man because he was considered a prodigy in his childhood, especially as he had won the Gold at the Junior World Championships. He then approached his coach for advice. His coach said that he needed to participate in another event to strengthen his body. His coach wanted him to run the 400-meter races.

The athlete instead wanted to run the 100-meter races. His coach felt that it was not advisable as his body type was not advantageous for the 100-meter sprint. Typically, 100-meter sprinters were shorter and stockier. This athlete was tall and lanky. He, however, convinced his coach to let him run the 100-meter races. He would run the 100-meter dash in the Beijing Olympics and run into worldwide fame with the world record timing of 9.69 seconds. He was Usain Bolt.

In Beijing, he went on to claim the Gold in the 200-meter and the 4x100-meter relay races as well.

He set world records in both these events. He would repeat this performance in the next two Olympics as well, winning the Gold in all three events. He succeeded in a race where conventional wisdom dictated that tall sprinters could not be fast as they were not fast starters. In a race that is completed within 10 seconds, a slow start is usually a losing cause. But Bolt was not deterred. He wanted to be the best, and he became the best.

Ten years before Bolt's heroics in Beijing, I found myself in Shanghai with a daunting challenge ahead as well. Before I reached Shanghai, I had failed in India. After my time at Bayer Agrochemicals, I got an opportunity to launch McCormick Spices in India. This was the opportunity of a lifetime. The biggest spice company in the world was entering the biggest spice market in the world. However, it did not take off in India (more on that later). I got an opportunity to redeem myself as McCormick wanted to enter the Chinese market.

The years 1990 to 2000 were known as the decade of the IT boom in India. People studied software engineering and related courses to go westward to the USA or to European countries searching for better education and careers. But I went East to Shanghai. I wanted to be a CEO by the age of 45. I saw the opportunity to go to China as one where I could separate myself from the pack.

"When the wind of change blows, some build walls, while others build windmills."

China might be India's neighbor, but it seemed like a different world. The language, the culture, and even the eating habits were completely different. This would be especially trying as I had moved along with my young family comprising of my wife and infant daughter.

We were among the first 50 families to ever move to Shanghai, China. This meant, we did not even have any established Indian families in the country to approach for any advice. In every sense of the word, our family had to be trailblazers in this part of the world.

The enormity of this challenge only struck me when I reached Shanghai. Thankfully, a couple of men in my team knew enough English to communicate with me. They were naturally apprehensive of me. However, they were generous in welcoming me. They offered me some tea and introduced themselves. An office boy had also rushed out and brought us each a plate of dumplings. My plate had a few fluffy dumplings, served on a base of chili oil. My new colleagues offered me a pair of chopsticks. Even as I was confused, I saw them use the chopsticks as pincers and roll the dumplings in the chili oil, thus coating the entire dumpling in fragrant and flavorful oil. They both ate it with great relish. Then they looked at me askance. I had to confess that I did not know how to use the chopsticks.

One of my colleagues then showed me. He asked me to open my hand. He placed one end of the chopstick on the base of my hand. He then asked me to slightly curve my fingers. He placed the other end on the side of my ring finger. Then he asked me to lay my thumb over the chopstick to hold it in place. He said it was vital that this chopstick remain stationary. He then picked the other chopstick and said that this was the top chopstick. I was asked to hold it between my thumb and index and middle fingers. He likened it to holding a pen or a pencil. I struggled with the holding. He then saw that my thumb was slightly crooked.

He pushed my thumb inward until it straightened. He said, "Your thumb has to be straight. If it is not straight, the bottom chopstick will fall down. Your thumb and the two fingers will serve as a fulcrum for navigating the food." He then demonstrated how the chopsticks could be used as pincers. I did not get it at the first try. However, I bravely carried on and tried to copy what they did. I could not hold on to the dumpling. But I used the chopstick to roll it around and coat it.

As I was trying to pick it up, I had a sudden thought. I asked, "Is this a dumpling with meat filling?" They nodded. I was shocked as I had been brought up as a vegetarian and I had never consumed meat. So, I laid the chopstick down and apologized for rejecting their generosity, and explained my dilemma.

I told them that I was a pure vegetarian and that I had not even eaten an egg. My colleagues were shocked. It was as if they had encountered an alien. They asked me how I could be a vegetarian when meat was so delicious. To this day, I am warmed by their hospitality. There was no judgment on my diet. They only held curiosity toward my choice of being a vegetarian. Soon we had a discussion going, and they wanted to know about the kind of dishes I usually ate. I explained to them how dishes like Masala Dosa and Poori were made among others. However, we had to start working soon.

One of the English speakers then said, "We will take you around Shanghai. This is your first day. You were able to arrive at the office because the office had arranged your transport. I am sure you have noticed that all the signs on the roads and shops are written in Mandarin. There are no English signs. Hence, today we will take you around and show you the city. You should familiarize yourself with the sights, the place, and the markets." I was grateful and accepted their kind offer.

Five of us bundled together in a colleague's car, and we went around. We started from the waterfronts, and I was shown some of the more impressive sights of the city. As we traveled, I was told of some of the more common phrases in Mandarin. Nǐ hǎo meant hello; Xièxiè meant thank you. So, they taught me some basic words to communicate. Soon, it was time for lunch. They asked me what I would want to have for lunch. I asked them to take us to a vegetarian restaurant and mentioned that I would pay for everyone's lunch. I thought of a quote by AD Posey: *"Good food warms the heart and feeds the soul."* I wanted to build good team spirit and providing lunch on the first day seemed like a good step in that direction. They gleefully accepted my offer.

We soon set out in search of a vegetarian restaurant. It seemed like an endless cruise. I saw the scenes change from my window. The tall buildings gave way to some of the more suburban sights. We stopped at almost every street. I then heard some furtive discussions as they pointed to each possible restaurant. Some restaurants were clearly serving non-vegetarian food as could be seen from the sausages and meats left outside after the curing process. In an effort to distract me, I was being entertained with some stories by my English-speaking colleagues.

They told me how Shanghai had developed over the past decade. They talked of how quickly the infrastructure had changed. And so, it went on! Soon, my stomach started rumbling. I looked at my watch and saw that it had been two hours since I had announced my intention to treat them to lunch. But we were still surfing the streets. I asked them, "Why have we not stopped for lunch yet? Do not tell me you are still trying to find an agreeable cuisine! Or are you worried about the prices?" One of my colleagues replied, "Sir, that is not the problem. We have been trying to find a vegetarian restaurant. All our restaurants serve non-vegetarian fare."

This was Shanghai in 1998. Today, a simple Internet search will help you find what you want. But it was a different world then, and I could only rely on word-of-mouth to find what I needed. My staff had never heard of a vegetarian-only restaurant. It was then that I realized the scale of my challenge. Even after two hours, we had not found a vegetarian restaurant. I knew I had to be the one to adapt. Otherwise, my team would keep endlessly surfing the streets of Shanghai to cater to my needs.

So, I asked them if anyone knew a vegetarian-only restaurant. When I received the answer that they knew of no such restaurant, I said, "Stop at the next restaurant. I will find a way to adjust." My colleague asked, "Are you sure? We can still look around." I replied, "No, we have not found one so far. We need to extend the time. I am sure all of you are hungry. I am sure I will find a vegetarian side dish." We stopped at a restaurant. The strong aromas and flavors wafted onto the street.

My colleagues seemed excited. I asked, "What is this restaurant? Why are they so excited?" The answer was, "This is a hotpot restaurant. Shanghai, this time of the year, begins to get cold. Hotpot restaurants are quite the 'hot spots' this time of the year. I hope you like spices. We love to eat spicy food." We entered the restaurant, and I was surprised by the layout of the place. The tables were circular and had a stove on top of them. Even considering the lateness of the hour, many tables were occupied with patrons having lunch. It seemed like a very communal affair. People were having fun and conversing in loud voices with one another.

We found ourselves a table, and we were all first served some tea. Then as my colleagues perused the menu card, I asked them if there were any vegetarian side dishes. They looked through the entire menu and could not find any item. Then they asked the server if there were any vegetarian side dishes. They had to explain to her that I was a vegetarian. People in the neighboring tables heard that comment. They looked at me as if I was a curious creature. One of them even reached out and patted my back and said something. I nodded in response and looked to my colleague to translate. He said, "The man has welcomed you to Shanghai. However, he also said that you would struggle here with the diet."

The server then said she would try to find something. Soon she came out with a stove. It had nine sections. Each had stocks of different shades of red color. I could understand that it was the spice level. I was then informed that the hotpot culture came from ancient China. It was meant to serve multiple people, and each section was supposed to cater to one person. My colleague continued, "That custom has not changed. These stocks are prepared using water, salt, and spices. And as you can see, each stock has its red chilies and peppercorns in them. However, in ancient China, the custom was not to dip your food into another's section as you did not want to get confused about whose food you were consuming. Now we decide which level of spice we would like, and we dip our meats within it. The rule is that once you dip your meat in one stock, you cannot dip it into another stock.

We do not want to mix the spice levels." Soon I saw the selection of meats come from the kitchen. The first item was served on a small bamboo pole. It had one section of its top layer removed. Within the hollow of the bamboo, there was an accumulation of some substance that was white. I asked them what was in the bamboo. They had a conversation to find the exact translation and then told me that it was shrimp. The shrimps were crushed into a paste. One of them asked around the table as to which spice level they wanted for their shrimp. When it was decided, they took a ladle and slid the shrimp right into the hotpot.

By this time, the stove was on, and the stocks were bubbling with the heat. The aromas of the boiling spices hit me immediately. Within 10-15 seconds, the chopsticks were out, and they enjoyed their bites. I could see from their facial expressions that they enjoyed it. Soon the server came out with two plates. She put one in front of me. It was a plate of peanuts. The other plate had some long noodles. However, they were flat, and I did not know what kind of noodles they were. It had some white color broth which meshed well with the white color of the noodles. I thought I could eat it with the dips and sauces which were at the side of the table. I asked my colleague if I could eat the noodles with soy sauce.

He was surprised. He asked me, "What noodles?" I pointed to the plate. He let out a loud laugh and let the others know of what I had said. I was confused. He then explained, "Do pardon me. I was not laughing at you. I just found the situation funny. Those are not noodles. They are duck intestines. He then took one intestine, and it was a long string-like substance. I could now see that it was not noodles. Each of them took an intestine and dipped it into their desired stock for another 10-15 seconds and then removed it and then coated it with the soy sauce and had a bite. I realized that the only vegetarian dish I could have for my lunch was a plate of peanuts. I poured some soy sauce on top of it and had my lunch. Meanwhile, my colleagues had a variety of meats, including beef, octopus, and fish. I only had a glass of orange juice after I consumed the peanuts.

Dinner was no better either. My wife has walked out during the day to find a good restaurant to have dinner. She, too, found no vegetarian-only restaurant. She also did not know the Mandarin language to shop for any ingredients. When I reached home that evening, we realized that we had no other choice. We had packed some biscuits and rusk from India. So, we made some tea and had it with biscuits and rusk. I knew that our diet was going to be one critical issue that would need to be resolved quickly. I looked into the mirror that night, and I was able to do so without any shame or guilt. Tea with biscuits and rusk was my breakfast fare as well the next day. My lunch was again a continuation of the previous day.

We went to a different restaurant, and my colleagues had a platter of seafood, and I had to make do with peanuts, soy sauce, and orange juice. Dinner was tea with biscuits and rusk. I had refilled our pantry with more biscuits and rusk after taking the assistance of my colleagues at the supermarket. I looked into the mirror that night, and I was able to look into the mirror without any shame or guilt.

The cycle continued. Breakfasts were copious amounts of tea and biscuits. Lunches were either eaten with my colleagues outside or they brought lunch from their homes. They got some variety. They provided me with bread, and some of them also gave me some vegetarian dishes like Mapo Tofu which was specially made for me. I packed these to take home and share with my wife. Otherwise, it was peanuts, soy sauce, and orange juice. Dinners were again the dishes given to me by my colleagues, or it was tea with biscuits. I could look into the mirror without guilt or shame. However, I noticed something else as well. I was becoming increasingly haggard. My diet was not good enough to keep me healthy.

It was at this juncture that I realized another challenge. I was trying to establish a company in a market consisting entirely of non-vegetarians. I was like a fish out of water. I was in a new country with no knowledge about its language and customs, and I was trying to sell products in a field in which I was inexperienced and did not have much knowledge of. I had to readjust myself if I wanted to succeed.

If I wanted to succeed in China, I knew I had to start by discarding my vegetarianism. I had to eat their food to know how to sell my company's products in the market. So, in my mirror test, I posed this question: If I started to have non-vegetarian food, would I be guilty or embarrassed to share my new dietary habits? My answer was that I would only experience those feelings if I kept it a secret.

So, the next day, I called my mother. I apologized to her and told her that I could no longer be a vegetarian. My mother was extremely wise, and she listened to my reasons and why it was important for me. She accepted my reasons and told me to do a good job. Then I surprised my colleagues by saying that I would eat the same food with them. They were stunned.

They knew that I had spent all my life shunning non-vegetarian food. They were moved by my efforts to integrate with them. I gave up a lifetime's worth of vegetarian diet to eat everything that flew, walked, crawled, and swam. I had embraced their culture. As I explored these new tastes and foods, I also noticed that my colleagues' apprehension toward me had disappeared as well. They would later reveal that when I had put in such an effort to integrate with them, how could they not reciprocate?

My next challenge was to learn how the Chinese ate their food. I had to understand their palate. I had to know how they used spices in their cooking. What were the dishes they preferred? How did they prepare their soups, appetizers, etc.?

These were the questions for which I urgently needed answers. I decided to find these answers in the kitchens of Chinese households. I visited forty different homes in forty days. I went into the kitchen as they prepared the food. I asked questions on how they made their dishes. Were there any variations they made according to the climate? What were those variations?

I asked them how different regions in China prepared different dishes. I found out that there were eight different types of Chinese cuisine: Anhui, Cantonese, Fujian, Hunan, Jiangsu, Shandong, Szechuan, and Zhejiang. All these cuisines had geographical and historical traditions behind them.

I sought to find the differences when I ate in Chinese homes. My efforts would not go unnoticed by my colleagues. They, too, made their efforts to help me settle down quickly. Our bonds would only go from strength to strength. It was not just from a personal standpoint. Professionally, too, we went from strength to strength. Within six years, we had carved out a space in the Chinese market for McCormick Spices.

We had made such rapid progress that I was promoted and asked to move to the headquarters in the USA. When my family and I went to the airport to fly to the US, 27 of my Chinese colleagues and their families had come to bid us farewell. We all had tears in our eyes, and it was an emotional send-off. If you were to take my personal journey and Bolt's 100-meter sprint in China, you will see one similarity.

We never intended to have success in that particular field. It was never an express aim. Bolt wanted to be a 200-meter Olympic champion, and I wanted to be a CEO for a global conglomerate in India. However, we stumbled on to a different path. Bolt would lose his only Olympic race in Athens, and I stumbled in establishing McCormick's presence in India.

We had to adapt to our failings and our new challenges. Bolt had to overcome a perceived physique issue for a 100-meter sprinter. I had to overcome a language barrier and discard a lifetime's worth of dietary habits. But we both did make a success of our efforts.

I would like to mention one of the thoughts that I will further elaborate on in the chapter on adaptability. Adaptability is about possessing the confidence and emotional fortitude to be calm and not yield to the circumstances. It is about being in the eye of what may seem like the fiercest hurricane.

It is about having the wit and wherewithal to be unruffled, and quick in thought and feet to manage expectations and priorities. But how do you become adaptable? What are the core skills involved in adaptability? If I were to distill my learnings from those six years in China, I would say these have been the most important:

1. **Communication skills:**
   Communication might seem easy. After all, we talk and listen to people every day. You might even say it is an essential human experience. However, it is a lot more complex than such an oversimplification. I only appreciated the finer details of this activity when I found myself in China. People spoke in Mandarin; the road signs and product labels too were in Mandarin. These symbols were like hieroglyphic characters.

   I had no previous familiar language insight. So, I had to learn the language. However, before I could learn the language, I had to lean heavily on non-verbal cues and other forms of communication. There was so much that I took for granted in this activity.

   This meant that I had to be an active participant in every conversation as I had to look for non-verbal cues and other gestures to communicate. It was only then that I realized that communication is far more than just speaking and listening.

2. **Interpersonal skills:**
   My efforts to integrate with my Chinese colleagues were welcomed wholeheartedly. They appreciated my adoption of their diet and my enthusiasm to learn Mandarin. They pitched in to help me do this faster. They welcomed me into their homes and answered my questions without reservation. We interacted positively and still remember one another as friends. I want to stress this point; when you try to integrate with others, they will reach back and help you adapt.

3. **Problem-solving skills/Creative thinking:**
   Whenever you find yourself in a new challenge, you can be overawed by the scale of the problem. Break these problems down into manageable issues.

When I came to China, I was burdened by my failure in India. However, I faced an entirely new set of problems in China. I had no notion of the country's palate, and the Internet was still in its infancy. So, while I had a slight idea of their eating habits, it was not enough for a marketing manager to sell spices. The most obvious solution would be to rely on my Chinese colleagues. But this was my remit. I had to find the solutions. This is why I started eating non-vegetarian food, as I knew I had to familiarize my tongue to their tastes. This is why I went into their homes and kitchens to find out more about their food.

This brings me to another question. Can anyone improve their adaptability? My answer is yes. However, there are a few things you should ensure if you want to improve your adaptability. The first thing is to be open to change. As the proverb said, do not build walls when you face the winds of change. If you do so, you will insulate yourself in an echo chamber where you will not be challenged. Therefore, it is important to have a mentality to grow. This means you have to be open to try new things even if it may scare you. I had to discard a lifetime's worth of vegetarian-only diet to adapt to the Chinese market.

Only when you have this mindset will you be open to change. The next important step is to set goals for yourself. I set a goal to understand Chinese cooking and cuisine in 40 days. So, I went into Chinese homes to learn. Some may argue that such behavior is not an example of determination. This is where I would like to differentiate between the meanings of two words: stubbornness and determination. The Oxford dictionary defines determination as firmness of purpose. It defines stubbornness as the dogged determination not to change one's attitude or position on something, especially in the face of good arguments or reasons to do so. My determination was in ensuring that McCormick would be successful in China. The next important step is to take feedback. Do not think of yourself as infallible. I, to this day, still look for feedback.

There is a Chinese proverb that goes thus: *He who asks a question is a fool for five minutes; he who does not ask a question remains a fool forever.* Therefore, when you find yourself in a new environment, always look for feedback.

Be aware of the changes in your domain. If you are working in a company, know what the company's policies and Standard Operating Procedures (SOPs) are. If you want to test the limits of your knowledge, first know the limits which you are allowed to test.

I would like to add that you should learn to acknowledge, accept, and love change as people tend to fear it instead. People like stability as it guarantees a level of comfort, and there is a lot that is desirable about stability, but people tend to over-exaggerate its benefits. I am not suggesting that you have to look for change constantly. I am only asking you to be open to it.

When you are open to change, you will find that your transitions will be smoother and your adjustments easier.

"Change is inevitable. Growth is optional." – John Maxwell.

It is at this juncture that I am reminded of the Choluteca Bridge in Honduras. Have you heard of the Choluteca bridge? The Choluteca bridge was built in the 1930s with the help of the USA in Honduras. It was an imitation of the Golden Gate Bridge. It connected the town of Choluteca with the rest of the country. Bridges are an important part of the Honduran economy as there are a lot of rivers in the country. So, in 1996, the Honduran government wanted to build a second bridge. Their reasoning was just, as Honduras is severely tested by nature. It is one of the five countries that make up the narrow landmass that connects two continents.

Honduras along with Guatemala, Costa Rica, Panama, and Nicaragua connects Mexico in North America and Colombia in South America. So, on one side, the country of Honduras has the Atlantic Ocean, and on the other side, the Pacific Ocean. Every year the country is wrecked by tropical storms and hurricanes. So, the Honduran government wanted to build a new bridge.

They sent out a global tender for the construction of a new bridge. A Japanese company by the name of Hazama Ando Corporation won the tender and constructed the bridge in 1998. The bridge was called the Bridge of the Rising Sun. However, it turned out to be a case of 'man proposes and nature disposes.' On 29th October, 1998, Hurricane Mitch made landfall in Honduras. It was a category five hurricane, the second deadliest Atlantic hurricane ever. Over 75 inches of rainwater was dumped in just over four days. Many bridges fell and were damaged. But the Bridge of the Rising Sun stood firm with minor damages. However, the roads connecting to the bridge were now washed away. The hurricane had caused the Choluteca River to carve a new channel for itself due to the flooding. Now the river no longer flowed under the bridge but around it.

The Bridge of the Rising Sun was now called the Bridge to Nowhere. Though the bridge was reconnected in 2003, there is a fundamental lesson to be learnt from the Choluteca Bridge. Whatever you have learned or whatever you feel you know will be rendered useless if you do not learn to adapt. IBM stayed and scoffed at the idea of smaller computers. Texas Instruments moved into that space, and they scoffed at the idea of personal computers, and Macintosh and Windows swooped into that market. Research in Motion (RIM) scoffed at the iPhone, and Google and Apple changed the market. They might have been fine institutions, but the world changed around them, and they were not ready.

Adaptability is an essential trait if you want to be a leader. In 2008, the Economist Intelligence Unit conducted a study, Growing Global Executive Talent. The aim of the study was to find what attributes were critical to be a good leader. Can you guess what the top three leadership attributes were? How high do you think technical skills ranked on the scale? Technical expertise was ranked among the least important skills, garnering only 10 percent of the surveyed votes. The three highest-ranked leadership abilities were motivating one's colleagues and staff; the ability to adapt and work with and across cultures; and finally, the ability to bring about change.

They garnered 35%, 34%, and 32% of the surveyed votes, respectively. This is an age where change is rapid and often complex. A pandemic savaged us, and terms like social distancing and work-from-home have become part of the daily lexicon. So, do not ever try to remain comfortable. Comfortable behavior leads to complacent behavior.

"All failure is failure to adapt, all success is successful adaptation."
– Max McKeown

8

ADAPTABILITY

"You must be shapeless, formless, like water. When you pour water in a cup, it becomes the cup. When you pour water in a bottle, it becomes the bottle. When you pour water in a teapot, it becomes the teapot. Water can drip, and it can crash. Become like water, my friend."
– Bruce Lee

Let me begin with two examples from the world of sports. Who is your favorite footballer? Depending on your affiliations, you could have different answers. Those of you who have watched many matches, depending on the era, might say Pele, Maradona, Ronaldo, Ronaldinho, Neymar, or even some of the young tyros like Mbappe and Haaland. But the sport has been headlined by two transcendent players in Cristiano Ronaldo and Lionel Messi. Just type in any of the aforementioned names on YouTube search. In response, you will find many compilations of their mazy dribbles, rainbow flicks, sombreros, rabonas, and fancy flicks and tricks set to chest-thumping music. You know that these tricks are just a small part of their game and not the core of their talent. However, even as you watch these highlights in awe, you would notice something peculiar. Cristiano Ronaldo's showboating will be found chiefly during his Manchester United and early Real Madrid days.

If you were to look at his more recent displays, they are about his athletic prowess. Just in 2020, there were many gasps of admiration when he leaped to meet a ball 2.56 meters from the ground with his head to score a goal. Cristiano Ronaldo has been a goal-scoring phenom with even age not slowing him down. This is not to get into the debate of who is better, Messi or Ronaldo.

But I have brought his example to highlight his adaptability. Even now, at the age of 36, when his agility and pace would not be equal to that of the young tyros of the game, he continues to stand at the top. It is not just down to the grizzled veteran's instinct honed over his career. It is about what he has done with it. He has distilled his game from being a flying, stylish, and tricky winger to one of the most lethal strikers in the game. He adapted his game to make his stay at the top of the game last longer.

Another sportsman I would like to bring up comes from the game of basketball. The year is 2009. Tall players dominate the game of basketball. Even today, height plays a decisive advantage in the game of basketball. Shaquille O'Neal is widely considered one of the most dominant big men in basketball history but is still playing in the NBA two years from retirement. He stood 7'1" tall. But in 2009, with the seventh pick in the NBA Draft, the Golden State Warriors have picked a 6'2" point guard. His name was Stephen Curry. This pick would bring a seismic change to the way basketball was played. Despite being the son of a former NBA player, Stephen Curry had to come through a less prestigious college to the pros.

In the same draft, the number one pick was a 6'7" power forward by the name of Blake Griffin. Griffin had made a name for himself as a ferocious dunker. Dunks were the calling cards of basketball players. Stephen Curry was limited in his ability to dunk due to his lack of elite athleticism and physique.

But he brought a new calling card. He was a three-point specialist. Sure, there were other three-point specialists before him like Reggie Miller or Ray Allen. But Curry was a different beast altogether. He could pull up anywhere from half-court to sink the ball into the basket.

He stretched defenses and after three NBA championships and two Most Valuable Player (MVP) awards, one of them being the only unanimous MVP in history, lately his game is now more about long-range shooting than finishing at the rim. At the time of writing, Blake Griffin has not won a single NBA championship. As for Curry, his size or athleticism did not limit him. He adapted, and then the game was forever changed.

So, what do you think of adaptability? It may be a word you might not have used very often. Or you may have come across it as a buzzword in management class or workshop. It is an essential skill for ensuring your health and happiness. If you were to think about it, we are very adaptable. If we go to a restaurant and order an item and find that it is not available, we immediately pick another one that is available. If you were commuting to the office and find the road blocked for some reason, you would look to find alternative options to reach your destination on time. However, these are minor speed bumps in daily life. How would you react, if say, you lose your job, or in the era of the COVID-19, you were to test positive for it? These are sudden roadblocks that are thrown at you. Adaptability is about adjusting to these sudden and massive changes. The year 2020 will be a significant point in the chronicles of human history.

This year has proved that the world can change rapidly, and what seemed to be under our control can be weaned away without warning. It is natural to be afraid of unforeseen circumstances. But to simply be afraid of the unknown is a waste of time and opportunity. Unknowns are fantastic learning opportunities for one to grow and mature. It is not just about learning to cope, but it is about shedding the shackles and thriving.

"When we least expect it, life sets us a challenge to test our courage and willingness to change; at such a moment, there is no point in pretending that nothing has happened or in saying that we are not yet ready. The challenge will not wait. Life does not look back. A week is more than enough time for us to decide whether or not to accept our destiny."
– Paulo Coelho.

Adaptability is about possessing the confidence and emotional fortitude to be calm and not yield to the circumstances. It is about being in the eye of what may seem like the fiercest hurricane. It is about having the wit and wherewithal to be unruffled, and quick in thought and feet to manage expectations and priorities. It is about optimism, to draw hope from the seemingly dire situation, and, as Bruce Lee remarked, to be water, no matter the circumstance.

Adaptability and Leadership

Every leader must be adaptable, especially if he wants to succeed in this multicultural world. Leaders are more likely to meet different kinds of people at the workplace. They can only earn the respect of their colleagues when they know how to motivate them to embrace change, make business operations smoother, etc. They can only do so when they are adaptable. Adaptability creates more happiness and overall life satisfaction.

Taking an example from nature, a caterpillar would never turn into a butterfly if it never adapts. So, if we refuse to embrace this skill, we will be stuck within the carapace of what we know and never fulfill our potential. The world has metamorphosed, and to survive, we need to break out of our cocoons and let our colorful wings unfurl and fly us to the new heights that were previously unattainable.

The world is no longer rigid. It is dynamic and demands that we be ready for change. It is like the oft-said adage, "The only thing predictable about life is that it is unpredictable." So, adapting to change is no longer optional but a necessity. Being adaptable is also important because it showcases your ability to be resourceful and displays your leadership skills, determination, analytical skills, and more. Leaders can develop adaptability by thinking out-of-the-box, stepping out of their comfort zone, and planning ahead. Adaptable leaders are those who are open and flexible in their approach. They look at challenges as opportunities to learn and, in some cases, even unlearn things.

Leaders rely on their experiences to navigate any new situation, but the best leaders will not allow their experience and ego to dictate their response. You can spot an adaptable leader when he/she is flexible and responds effectively to the circumstance, even if their plans lie in tatters. They lead the team with effective communication and keep the morale up. They will not let people dwell on the negatives but reflect on the learnings from the failures.

You do not need me to tell you that our world is changing. We went from having paper and file, brick and mortar companies to the digital landscape within couple of decades. The year was 2007, and the following was a conversation between two people. One said, "These guys are really, really good. This is different." The other replied, "It's okay. We will be fine." This might seem like an innocuous conversation. But what if I add some context to the conversation?

The first person was Mike Lazaridis, and the other was Jim Balsillie. Those who belong to the tech world would have now known the gravity of the conversation. For those of you yet to grasp the death knell that this conversation was, I will provide you with more context. They were the co-CEOs of a company called RIM which produced a phone called Blackberry. At this point, Blackberry held 50% of the smartphone market in the USA and 20% in the world. They had this conversation after watching one Steve Jobs announce a revolutionary product called iPhone.

The iPhone did not just affect Blackberry. At this point in time, Nokia was the leader when it came to phones. Nokia was an early mover and the market share leader with a substantial cost position. But Apple came in with an adaptive system of suppliers, telecom partnerships, and independent application developers. Google also adopted this model with its Android operating systems.

All these changes led Nokia's CEO Stephen Elop to address his staff in a memo which read, "Our competitors aren't taking our market share with devices; they are taking our market share with an entire ecosystem." These are not the only examples of companies failing to adapt. In 1977, one company patented the digital camera.

Even as the traditional camera that used film dominated the market, one company decided to patent the digital camera. Can you guess which was this company? Could it be Canon? Or Nikon, Fujifilm, Panasonic, or Sony? You will recognize all these names. They are among the leading digital camera makers in the world. But the first company to patent the digital camera was Kodak. However, they decided to stay put as the film camera made them a lot of money, and they ignored the digital camera. They stuck to it even when the market shifted toward the digital market. They failed to adapt even as their competitors did.

These may be examples of companies failing to adapt. But there are also many examples of companies adapting to the changing landscape to thrive. Jimmy Iovine is one of the most legendary music producers. His record label, Interscope Records, brought artists like Dr. Dre, Eminem, Kendrick Lamar, Lady Gaga, Gwen Stefani, and Selena Gomez to the world. But at the dawn of the new century, Iovine was faced with a new problem. The world was waking up to the many advantages of the Internet. The Internet brought a new challenge, piracy. People could now resort to downloading music for free. The records were not selling as well.

Iovine did turn to the legal authorities and the law to combat this problem. But this was like putting a Band-Aid on a bullet hole. Then Iovine embraced digital change. He met with a few people from tech. He met two particular people and thought, "Oh, this is where the party is. We need to incorporate this thinking into Interscope." The two people were Steve Jobs and Eddy Cue from Apple. This partnership would launch iTunes.

Let us examine the hierarchy within a company. Let us say that a middle manager has left a company. The company does not headhunt for the position from the outside. Instead, a supervisor is promoted from within the company. Do you think the supervisor will have the same remit? Indeed, the scope of his job has increased, and his responsibilities would have become more complex. He will need to change his style of work. He may need to be more subtle or more persuasive based on the circumstances.

He may also have to abandon some practices from his earlier position. For example, his previous position would have allowed for some form of micromanagement. But in his new position, he will have to trust his team, and as he would now not have any time to micromanage. He will have to learn to trust, delegate, and foster allies.

"Action & Adaptability create opportunity." – Garrison Wynn

If you never adapt, you will never know what your capabilities are. Perhaps you may find something truly worth doing. You discover something new within you. You may never have had the faintest idea till now, but you could learn a new skill that you would probably be really good at. Virender Sehwag has been one of the most devastating openers in the history of cricket. He was flamboyant and ruthless, and came to define the 21st century of Indian cricket as he won a T20 World Cup and a 50-over World Cup. His swashbuckling innings had played a crucial part in both those campaigns and resulted in many memorable victories for India. However, he used to be a lower-middle-order batsman with no credible prospects to make it to the Indian national team.

Then Saurav Ganguly asked him to open the innings. He persuaded him to open even when Sehwag displayed his reluctance. But in 2002, Ganguly would ensure that Sehwag opened the innings and the rest, as they say, is history. If Sehwag had not adapted, cricket would have never seen one of its brightest luminaries. You could also learn from Amitabh Bachchan. When he entered Bollywood, his first few films were considered commercial flops. He then adapted the role of the angry working-class young man into his film roles in movies like Sholay and Deewar. He transitioned himself and morphed into different characters. He adapted himself and became one of the finest actors the world has ever seen. He broadened his range and scope. He did not allow himself to be typecast. Contrastingly, look at someone like Sylvester Stallone. He can be traced to the first muscleman action hero with Rambo.

However, he is still being cast in movies that need him to be the same hero, or that strike a similar nostalgic note. But when you study Amitabh Bachchan's roles, you find him playing different characters in films like Piku and Pink. So, you too should be ready to adapt. Now, do you wish to be a manager or a leader who is dependable and admirable? I have a few suggestions on how you can improve and build on your adaptability.

1. **Learn:**
   The first step is to recognize that you are human. There is no chance that you will have all the answers. When you assume an egoistic position that you have all the methods, you will fail. So, be curious. When you do not know something, admit it and ask questions to fill in your knowledge gaps. When you involve others, you will find that problem solving becomes easier. You will find that fresh perspectives will give you ideas that you had not considered before. So, in the words of Shetty Teacher, educate yourself.

2. **Be wary of your inner monologues:**
   What are you telling yourself? If there is something that can paralyze you from acting, it is to doubt yourself. When you cast doubts on yourself, you will constantly second-guess your moves. A leader needs to be bold. So, be confident in yourself and do not let your inner doubts plague your mind.

3. **Step outside your comfort zone:**
   This idea is in the same vein as educating yourself. When you enter a new phase, you will naturally be wary. The only way you can rid yourself of these early nerves is to challenge yourself constantly. Step outside your comfort zone. When you dare to go beyond what you assumed was possible, you will see a whole new world with all its possibilities open up to you.

4. **Take small steps forward:**
    In the current environment, the best strategy is one in which you use what you know right now to determine just your very next step. When you take that step, check for the result and let that determine the next small step. Small steps in an unknown territory allow for easy course correction.

5. **Show yourself some compassion:**
    Not every step will have the intended result. Know that it is okay. Not every step is meant to take you across the finish line. The race is won by an accumulation of steps. Rather than spending any time beating yourself up, look instead at what you might learn that will inform your next move.

"It is not the strongest of the species that survives, nor the most intelligent that survives. It is the one that is most adaptable to Change."
– Charles Darwin

This quote by Darwin will surely remind you of the famous picture of human evolution. It starts from the left, where an ape is walking on all its four legs, to the right, where it evolves into the *Homo sapiens* species of today. The *Homo sapiens* species survived because they adapted and evolved. The 1980s and 1990s saw the dominance of Smith Corona. It was a company that produced typewriters. They became the leaders in the technology related to typewriters like grammar checkers, laptop word processors, and built-in dictionaries. If you notice the trend, you will see that they had the opportunity to transition into personal computers and word processing. But they did not pull the trigger, and it is no longer a name that most people remember. If you were to look at computers, IBM was the leading manufacturer at one point. But they dismissed the idea of personal computers. Now they are no longer a major player in the hardware business. But they adapted to the mistake. They adapted, evolved, and transitioned into hosting and consulting services, and have now become market leaders in those services.

With the onset of the pandemic, you may have seen the usage of applications like Google Pay, Paytm, and PhonePe skyrocket. Why is that? Banks used to be the primary way to dispense cash for transactions. But banking has been weighed down by its inherited legacy systems. The new-age phones are digitally way ahead of these old systems. So other players stepped into this space. If you were to notice it, adaptability is not just about the reaction. It also asks you to be proactive. Anticipate for change and be ready for it. Only when you look to be proactive can you effectively be reactive.

In closing,

1. It does not matter if you are skilled; it does not matter if you are qualified; it does not even matter if you are experienced; if you are not adaptable all of those aforementioned qualities will not help you reach your potential. Be willing to embrace the unknown. It will be the making of you. Confront your challenge with confidence and optimism, and you will find it easier.

2. People will take note when you are adaptable. It will be proof that you are wise beyond your years. It will be evidence that your capabilities lie far beyond what your current role is within your company. It is an indication of your strengths—to be unruffled by any challenge and the ability to morph your methods to the situation—that can help your company win.

3. When you are adaptable in your career, you also show that you are a thinker with forethought. It shows that there is a constant quest to improve and know beyond what you may already know. It shows control and curiosity even when it comes at the cost of a comfortable, professional path.

"Life isn't about waiting for the storm to pass. It's about learning how to dance in the rain."
—Vivien Greene

PART C: YOU TOO CAN DO IT

9

NO PAIN, NO GAIN

If your determination is fixed, I do not counsel you to despair. Few things are impossible to diligence and skill. Great works are performed not by strength, but perseverance."
— Samuel Johnson

The year was 1977. A 15-year-old boy named Rick asked his father, Dick Hoyt, to help him run a five-mile race. He wanted to do this to benefit a lacrosse player in his school who had become paralyzed. Rick Hoyt was diagnosed with cerebral palsy at birth. His father, then 36, was never a runner. After their first race, Rick commented that when they ran, he did not feel disabled. So, his father started training when his son went to school. He ran with a bag of cement on a wheelchair. They would one day run a 5-mile race in 17 minutes. However, that would not be the limit of their achievements. Do you know what an Ironman Triathlon is? A triathlon is a multidiscipline race that involves running, swimming, and cycling over various distances. As the name suggests, Ironman Triathlons are among the most demanding endurance sports events in the world. They have a time limit of 16–17 hours for completion. The event typically starts at 7 am. They begin with a 2.4-mile (3.86 km) swim. There is a mandatory cut-off time of 9:20 am.

Dick would swim this event with a special boat carrying his son tied to him. The next stage of the triathlon is a 112-mile (180.25 km) bicycle race. The mandatory cut-off time for this stage is 5:30 pm. Dick would race this stage with his son on a seat at the front of the bicycle. The final stage of the triathlon is a marathon 26.22-mile (42.20 km) run. The cut-off time for this race is midnight. Dick Hoyt pushed his son on a wheelchair for this stage. If you do not complete any of the stages within the cut-off time, you could not finish the race. The pair would go on to complete six such Ironman Triathlons.

Perseverance is essential if you want to succeed in life. I first got the chance to plant McCormick's flag in India in the 1990s. I built an excellent team to help launch the company. We did our research and committed long hours to ensure its success. We marketed products like cumin seeds, turmeric powder, coriander powder, etc. We found that most of these spices were sold 'loose.' Even the packaged products were drab in their presentation. Once we had carried out our meticulous research, we started work on identifying the suppliers. We studied and traced the source of the more successfully sold spices.

We then went and negotiated with these suppliers for large quantities of spices. Next, we hired a few designers to design some beautiful packets. We wanted to make sure that our design would grab the attention of the customers when they walked into a store. We adopted this method because all research pointed to the fact that people responded to imagery better. We were also confident about our products. It is not enough if people are attracted by the design, but end up with a sub-standard product. However, we made one critical error. Our products were meant to stand out on the shelves of a supermarket.

The problem was that the concept of supermarkets was still a foreign one in the Indian consumer consciousness in 1998. People still looked to the neighborhood store for their needs. The products failed to take off despite our best efforts. Then I got the opportunity to go to Shanghai. Even as I succeeded in China and in the USA, there was always this sticking point.

I wanted the biggest spice company in the world to mark its presence in the biggest spice consuming market in the world, which is India. However, McCormick was unsure about returning to India and starting from scratch. I started working with McCormick's Merger & Acquisition team to identify a company that McCormick could take over and through which they could make a mark in the Indian market. We identified a renowned spices company in south India and acquired stakes in this company. A year later, McCormick acquired a reputed food brand in north India. Our team worked hard to ensure that the second time was the charm. Ten years after the failure of the first launch, I was able to plant the flag of McCormick in India finally.

Helen Keller said it best when she said, "A bend in the road is not the end of the road...unless you fail to make the turn." I was never discouraged by my first failure. It only fueled my drive to ensure that the second time would be a success. Think of the summit of any mountain. How do you get there? It needs effort and desire. You cannot just wish to be there. It requires your steadfast commitment to the goal. The road to success is often paved with many failures. It can tempt you into giving up. Progress can be slow. Perseverance is what will keep you moving. It is also contagious. When your staff see you driven even in the face of failure, they too will be inspired to dream and to dare.

In the previous chapter, I talked about how I founded the alumni association of my school. I had founded a prior iteration of school alumni 20 years back before I went abroad. We were a group of friends who wanted to do good within our community. We had worked during the monsoon season with buckets and drained the standing water accumulated within our school premises. I always remembered Shetty Teacher's advice. I wanted to ensure my alma mater did not need its students to spend their time on other activities at the cost of time which could have been spent studying. We fundraised to help build drainage solutions within the school. When we finished our education, we tried to bring our expertise and contacts to help the community.

When I started working at Bayer, I managed to make some contacts within the local medical community. My friends and I helped to organize some vaccination drives and medical camps for our communities.

As a child, my favorite get-together within the community involved the festivals of Diwali, Holi, and Janmashtami. When I became an adult, my favorite get-togethers were the many events we organized for our community, like the book camps and medical camps. We also started regular exercise and walking clubs for the senior members of our community. However, when I moved to China, I lost touch with these activities. My friends also lost touch with the association when their careers and lives took them in different directions.

When I visited my school during Guru Poornima, I managed to bring people together to provide drinking water for the school. I had to return to the USA after that. Some of my friends did manage to organize some more events for the community. However, they were still functioning informally. When I finally moved back to India, I joined them. We then reached out to our mutual friends and others to rekindle the association. Now I had the time to accompany my friends to conduct a far more extensive campaign to contact the alumni of our school. Our efforts were not wasted. Many more people responded back, and we were able to do a lot more for our community. We all were enthusiastic about the possibilities. We found that some students could not afford smartphones to participate in classes that were held remotely due to the lockdown during the recent pandemic.

Someone suggested that we provide these people with smartphones. We ran a fundraiser and raised enough funds to buy smartphones and help students attend classes. Before the pandemic, we had organized many more health camps and book camps. All it took was just a spark, and now a 1000 of us in the association are always looking to better the lives of our school students in the areas of education and infrastructure. There is something contagious about perseverance. I experienced something similar in China.

My family was among the first 50 families to immigrate from India to Shanghai, China as I mentioned before. Soon, we had a lot more Indians immigrating to China. Some of us who had been living in China for the past four years knew the kind of troubles these newly arriving Indians would face. We decided to form an association for the newcomers. Our aim was to provide networking and help them navigate Shanghai. We wanted to help acclimatize the new employees or businessmen to the rules and laws of the land. We also offered help in terms of 'whom to approach' and 'how to approach them' in case of any issues or emergencies. It was called the Shanghai Indian Business Association (SHIBA). Our wives also wanted to form a support organization for the women. My wife knew the early troubles she had faced with grocery shopping. Even though I had started eating non-vegetarian food, she remained a vegetarian. So, she was keen to help other women navigate Shanghai and provide them with information about where to go for groceries.

It was called the Shanghai Indian Ladies Association (SHILA). In 2002, I knew that these organizations were doing a lot of work that overlapped each other. I saw that there was an opportunity to do better. I suggested that we combine both the associations. I was met with skepticism. I understood their apprehension. This was a time when China did not allow a gathering of more than 20 people at a time. I remember one year when we were celebrating Holi. People looked at us suspiciously. A policeman saw us celebrating and approached us, and questioned us about our celebrations. He even pointed to the *tilaks* on our foreheads and enquired about it. So, people were very apprehensive about combining both the associations.

However, I was able to convince everyone of the benefit of having a single association to represent Indians in Shanghai. Later, we successfully formed the 'Indian Association' in Shanghai in the year 2003, and I had the privilege to be its Founding President. We carried out several activities and conducted several events for the benefit of Indians living in China. Today the association has grown bigger and better.

This association had an opportunity to host our honorable Prime minister Narendra Modi for an exclusive session with Indians in Shanghai in 2018. I want you to consider these cases:

1. An aspiring basketball player was cut from his high school basketball team. He was shattered. He went home, and locked himself in his room and cried. The boy would go on to win 6 NBA titles and would go down in history as one of the greatest, if not the greatest, to play the game of basketball. His name: Michael Jordan.

2. A young child was not able to speak until he was almost four years old. He was not thought to be academically gifted. His teachers even remarked that he would not amount to much of anything. The boy would become a theoretical physicist and also a Nobel laureate. He was Albert Einstein.

3. A woman was demoted from her job as a news anchor as the network bosses deemed that she was not fit for television. The woman would go on to become one of the most recognizable names in television and launch her own network. She was Oprah Winfrey.

4. A writer was sacked from his job at a newspaper. He was told that he lacked imagination and that he had no original ideas. The boy launched an empire that would involve cartoons, movies, and even theme parks. He was Walt Disney.

5. Another young boy faced the cruelty of sport when he was cut from his team at the age of 11. He had a more diminutive stature compared to his peers, and he was diagnosed with a growth hormone deficiency. The boy with the deficiency of growth hormone would later be known to the world as Lionel Messi.

6. An entrepreneur, at the age of 30, was sacked from the company he founded. He would be left depressed and devastated. He would return to the company with his head held high. He would also go down as one of the most

creative entrepreneurs in history. His name: Steve Jobs.

7. A young boy with no father figure and a mother with drug abuse issues struggled with the constant moving. He would drop out of high school and have his own personal struggles with poverty and drug abuse. The high-school dropout would become one of the most successful musicians of his time and would be known to the world as Eminem.

8. A pleasant young boy was known to be polite to everyone. However, he did not seem to be academically gifted. A teacher even told him that he was too stupid to learn anything. He was advised to go into a field where his personality would help him succeed. The boy who was told that he would not succeed would bring light to the world via an incandescent bulb. He was none other than Thomas Edison.

9. Four young Scousers went to a studio company called Decca Recording Studios to get a record deal. They were rejected and told that they did not sound good and that they had no future in show business. The four Scousers as a group became a chart-topping success in the United Kingdom (UK) and the USA and would become the sound of a generation. They were the Beatles.

10. A man tried his hand at stand-up comedy and was booed off the stage at his first attempt, and at the age of 15, he had to take up the job of a janitor to support his family. The 15-year-old janitor would become one of the finest comedians and actors in the world. We know him as Jim Carrey.

11. A single mother's first manuscript had been rejected by 12 major publishers. She was left in poverty and was on welfare. This single mother would charm the 21st century with her Harry Potter series of books. She was JK Rowling.

12. A 62-year-old man was broke, but he had an idea. He pitched it to over 1000 restaurants, and all of them rejected him. He would start one of the most iconic fast-food restaurants in the world, KFC. He was Colonel Sanders.

What do you see that is common to all these cases? They were all called failures. Those of you who are well-read will probably already know about these people. There are countless examples of people who failed initially, but eventually became successful due to their persistence and drive.

There will be roadblocks in your life. Will you consider them as walls that limit you, or will you see them as hurdles you are meant to soar over? My company, every year, holds an annual get-together event for all the employees. You can call it an annual day where we come together, take stock, celebrate, and look towards the future. As the head of the company in India, I am given the responsibility to open the event. I could have given speeches. But I wanted to be different. Every year I did something new. It was not just for the novelty, but it was also a challenge I took it upon myself to learn something new every year.

This past year I decided to play the piano. Did I have a musical background? No. I could not tell one note from another. But I was determined to learn. My wife even told me that at the age of 54, it was not necessary for me to do this. Anyone who has learned a musical instrument will know the struggle I underwent. There were days when I wanted just to throw my fingers at the keys in frustration. There were days when I was exasperated that I could not learn one single song. There were days when I felt like I had not improved even an iota. But practice, I did. There was a day when I was able to play one verse haltingly. It was a good day. I was reminded of a time when the Bollywood actor Boman Irani surprised people when he played the guitar at the IIFA Awards in 2010. He had made some comedic remarks about his struggle to learn the guitar.

One joke that remains in my head is about how Irani supposedly asked his teacher when he would be ready to play 'Hotel California', and his teacher answered back that he was not even prepared for a rendition of 'Baa, Baa, Black Sheep.' However, I never slacked a single day. I had allocated a couple of hours every day to practice the piano.

Even on the bad days, I put in the effort. Finally, on the day of the event, the video opened with someone's fingers playing the piano. The tune was familiar. It was a Bollywood classic. Even as people hummed the tune or sang the lyrics, the camera panned out to show me playing the piano.

This was no gimmick. I learned how to play that song, and I succeeded in playing it live to my audience. There will be occasions when you feel like you have hit a plateau. It will be easier to quit. But keep at it. Sooner or later, that plateau will turn into a springboard. Kobe Bryant, who was famed for his work ethic, was asked how he mentally prepared himself for any failure. He said that he would tell himself, "Get over yourself." He would tell himself that if he shot five airballs, and if he feels that people would look at him differently, he would tell himself to get over himself. He was not that important. Then he would rationally look at those five airballs and analyze why the ball did not reach the basket. He would see that the line was perfect, but the length was not there. He would find the cause to be a lack of strength and stamina. Accordingly, he would then work toward building that strength and stamina.

Look at the most extraordinary people in the world. Most of them seem the same as you. They were not born with some prodigious talent. There could be some of them who were born with an innate gift in a particular field. But there are an equal number of gifted people who never made it. But extraordinary people have one thing in common. They held on. They held on in the face of dire circumstances. They held on even as they failed. They held on even as they would have been mocked. They held on even as they learned something from every setback. They held on until they became successful.

"The only guarantee for failure is to stop trying."
– John C Maxwell.

If you want to reach a goal, it can be tough to remain determined. It can be a long and arduous path. Keep at it.

The way you can cultivate perseverance is to know your goal. If you are not sure of what you want, you will never be able to persevere. You can work hard even if you are not sure of what you want in life. But to persevere, you need a goal. Commitment demands desire. I had the desire to be a CEO by the age of 45, and I achieved it.

I had the desire to plant the flag of the biggest spice company in the world in the biggest spice market in the world. I failed once. I returned to it, and I succeeded. Although you have an endgame in sight, keep some short-term goals. Knock them off and set new goals. Keep drawing and redrawing new lines. Keep doing them until you achieve your long-term goals. It is as APJ Abdul Kalam said, "If four things are followed—great aim, acquiring knowledge, hard work, and perseverance—then anything can be achieved."

Do not be discouraged by pain. You may mistakenly think of it as punishment or humiliation. It is instead a time for reflection. You will never get things granted to you. You need to put in the effort. Even when the Gods granted boons to people, it was a result of their penance and perseverance. To really appreciate what you have earned, it is important to have put in the effort. When we commit physically and/or emotionally to gain something, it becomes much more valuable. They stick with us longer because it would have taught us the value of our hard work. It will have granted us unique perspectives and insights in our pursuit. It is from the pain that we learn, mature, and grow. It reveals our hidden potential. It pushes us out of our comfort zone and helps us to evolve as people.

"I learned patience, perseverance, and dedication. Now I really know myself,
and I know my voice. It's a voice of pain and victory."
– Anthony Hamilton

10

BE DIFFERENT; NOT ME TOO

"The person who follows the crowd will usually go no further than the crowd. The person who walks alone is likely to find himself in places no one has ever seen before."
– Albert Einstein

If you want to succeed in life and achieve your dreams, there is one thing you should always remember. Be different; do not follow the crowd. Find your Unique Selling Proposition (USP) and unleash it to your advantage. Think of the most successful people and companies; they became successful because they separated themselves from the pack. *Mogambo khush hua* has to be one of the most iconic lines in Indian cinema. Even if people had not watched the movie *Mr. India*, they would immediately recognize that particular line of dialogue as it has been immortalized in the film lore of this country. Why did the line become so iconic? It was because of the charisma and gravity with which that line was delivered. When Amrish Puri burst onto our screens with that line, we believed it because of the deep base voice. His magnetic voice made us look past the perceived deficiencies of the actor.

While Amrish Puri was a phenomenal hero, his pockmarked face and dusky complexion meant he could never be an A-list protagonist in Bollywood. But he knew the value of his voice. He leveraged it to become an A-lister and one of the celebrated antagonists of Indian cinema. He transformed what seemed his deficiencies into one of his strengths. It is all about what you do with what you have and not lamenting about what you do not have.

One of the greatest disservices you can do to yourself is to compare yourself to others and be discouraged by thinking about what you lack. We could also do greater damage to ourselves when we think something makes us abnormal. We try to mask it and keep it hidden. Maya Angelou said it best when she said, *"If you are always trying to be normal, you will never know how amazing you can be."* I will encourage you to celebrate your differences. They make you special. Own it as it is not easy to be different from others. Our education and training have meant that we study the same courses and we are trained for the same roles. You have to be the cream that rises to the top. Just like Maya Angelou said, find out how amazing you can be.

I want you to reflect on the fact that there are close to 7 billion people in this world. How will you distinguish yourself from others? Think of yourself as a brand. How did the most successful brands leave their mark in this world? I trace their success to three essential components:

1. They are extremely good at practicing their values.
2. They stand out from the rest and stand clear of the field as the best.
3. Their communication is comprehensive. They effectively communicate their values and how they are better than the rest.

If you want to be successful, you too have to examine yourself based on these components. Why do I stress the importance of being different? If you have ever attended a job interview, one of the more common questions you could face is this:

What makes you unique? It may seem like a cliched question. However, that question is asked for a reason. When you describe your alma mater, how do you describe it? You call yourself a product of a certain college. For example, if you graduated from an IIM, you would proudly strut, calling yourself an IIM graduate. However, if you were very perspicacious, you will realize that many others have equally impressive backgrounds. You have now become a commodity. You have lost your specialty when you are placed with people from the same background.

One of the best things you can do to yourself is to embrace yourself, warts and all. If you think you are limited by something, it is your thinking which is limited. Have you heard of the fearsome foursome? They were tearaway pace bowlers in cricket from the Caribbean who terrified batsmen everywhere with their speed and bounce. They were Andy Roberts, Michael Holding, Colin Croft, and Joel Garner. However, India too possessed a foursome of great repute. They were the spin quartet of Bhagwat Chandrasekhar, Bishen Singh Bedi, Srinivas Venkataraghavan, and Erapalli Prasanna. They played a vital part in some of our early victories abroad, even as we were finding our foot in the world of cricket.

Within that quartet, I would ask you not to look any further than Bhagwat Chandrasekhar. If you knew your cricket trivia, you would know that he holds one of the rare records of having more wickets than runs scored. But I want to focus on his supposed deficiency. At the age of five, he was struck down by polio. He would lose feeling in his right hand. So, he grew up playing sports like badminton and table tennis with his left hand.

He did try various therapies to rejuvenate his right hand. None of them worked until he picked up a leather ball. It was a cricket ball. He would find out that he could deliver it far too quickly for a spinner. Soon he discovered that he was greatly effective as a leg spinner. If you watch any match highlights of Chandrasekhar, you will see him run up to the crease like a medium-pacer and throw down balls with great topspin and googlies that would outfox batsmen.

He never regained the strength in his right hand, but he turned it into a match-winning weapon. It was not just that he overcame such a barrier to be a match-winner for India. His presence automatically motivated his teammates to be better. Chandrasekhar, the mystery spinner, turned a deficient arm into an advantage with which he bamboozled his opponents.

"When you are like everyone, you are nobody; but when you are different from everyone, you are somebody.
- Mehmet Murat ildan

Let us look back at the last 20-30 years in Bollywood. Based on that history, if you were to construct a model Bollywood hero, what would you do? Will you look at the romantic charmer in Shahrukh Khan with his arched back and extended arms? Would you look at the great dancers like Hrithik Roshan and Ranbir Kapoor? Would you look at the action films filled with catchy one liners featuring Salman Khan and Akshay Kumar? If you were to peruse these actors and their roles, you would see many similarities. You cannot really address any specific genre to any of these heroes. They could interchange their roles and portray it equally well.

However, in their midst was one of India's finest actors. Irrfan Khan essayed characters who were the epitome of the everyday man. While the blockbuster actors chose roles larger than life, Irrfan Khan imbues his characters with everyday grace and honesty. You cannot imagine of any of the superstar actors pulling off the same role with similar élan. He could not dance, so he did not sell his performances based on any song or dance. He even embraced his non-dance skills in a hilarious sketch that parodied Bollywood party songs.

He did not flex his muscles or show six-pack abs. He did not glamourize his roles. Even when he essayed roles in Hollywood films, he did it with the same grace. He became one of India's greatest stars by simply defying the rule. He carved a space for himself and became a trailblazer. In an example much closer to home, there is the case of the Kannada film industry.

It was once dominated by actors like Rajkumar, Vishnuvardhan, and Ambareesh. They all played roles of virtuous family men. Kiccha Sudeep burst onto the scene as an angry, tall young man and blazed a path for himself. Even in the world of make-believe and superstars, people found a way to blaze their own path. Irrfan Khan and Sudeep did not do anything new. They just found their strengths in what made them different from the type. We are social creatures. So, it is natural that we want to belong somewhere. However, you can sometimes damage your potential when you lean too much to fit in. When you look to fit in, you look externally for fulfillment. You look for approval from others for finding value in yourself. When you get into this habit, all your relationships will be tainted.

Even when you look for partners, you will look for partners who can provide you with the worth you cannot provide for yourself. You will look for material comforts. You will be struck with a perpetual fear of missing out. You will scour social media posts and see the seemingly fabulous life of other people. You will be looking to do the same. If you were to notice, most of these activities involve you doing something for happiness and finding your worth.

None of these activities involve you being you. The consequence is that you are no longer living your own life. You are living the life dictated by others. Your likes are determined by others. This will not provide you with happiness. Any joy will be transient and elusive. You will always be chasing the next thing for happiness. Such a pursuit is endless and will bear no fruit. When you live your life based on the idea of what others deem as acceptable, you will only live up to a fraction of what you are capable of.

After all, how can you be genuinely happy if you are not genuinely you? Never be Me Too for other people to like you. Trust yourself. Be you, even if it makes you different. I can guarantee that when you are true to yourself, the right people will find you. You will attract them with your authenticity. So, how can you be different? I will answer this question on two fronts, personal and professional. It will not be easy to embrace yourself, warts and all if you are looking to fit in with the others.

First, you should open yourself. Remember, this is your life. Therefore, even at the cost of any immediate angst, you must look to find your uniqueness. When you look in that direction, you will soon find that any purposelessness or anxiety you had will slowly start melting away. The next step would be to identify your bad habits. Ask yourself if you look to seek approval from others. If your answer is yes, inquire what you should do to find that approval from yourself.

Do you find yourself dreary and dissatisfied? Inquire of yourself what you need to get out of that state of being. Which activities in your day fill you with dread? Which activities do you find yourself procrastinating about? Are there any activities that you would rather not do, but you do them just to fit within a clique? Demand answers to these questions from yourself. These answers will lay out in stark detail how much you have deviated from yourself.

The next step would be to identify something that you really want to do. If you remember, I had the ambition to be a CEO by the age of 45. That aim dictated my life and the decisions I took. When people were moving to the USA or to Europe for better opportunities, I knew I had to go to China. It was the place where I had to distinguish myself.

My ambition gave me energy when I needed it the most. I remember my internship when my fellow interns and I were given an assignment. We were supposed to go and interview people in the medical business, chiefly doctors, about a 5-star hospital. We were supposed to survey them for the feasibility and attractiveness of the project. I was placed in Bangalore.

My fellow interns were placed in other metropolitan cities. This was an era when the STD/ISD phone booths were popular. We were supposed to draw up a business plan based on the survey. I was driven by the need to be the best. I had no idea about the progress of my friends.

I decided that I would do my best. I worked on the project by going to the doctors' early morning jogging haunts to interview them, and I worked till 10 pm every day.

When the internship was over, I realized that I had interviewed over four times the number of doctors that my friends had interviewed. It was this passion that helped me outwork my friends.

While my workday might seem hectic, I enjoyed my work and pushed through. I realized my difference that day. I was driven and ambitious, and had the work ethic attached. I could have slacked on any given day or become worried by irrational fears. So, find out what makes you unique. You may not find the answer immediately. Take your time and focus on your uniqueness. Keep a notepad beside you and write down what you think. List down the activities during which you do not feel the passage of time. What are the activities that you unfailingly do even if you are short on time? What are the things that matter to you? What is it that makes you happy? One final question I want you to answer is to find which values define you. Which are the values that you cannot compromise on? List these answers down and reflect on the answers. They should reinforce your uniqueness to yourself. Once you have the answers you need, evaluate how much of these answers are aligned with your life. They will let you know if you have masked yourself and hidden away the real you.

The next step would be to leverage these answers and realign your life. Follow the examples of Amrish Puri and Chandrasekhar. I am reminded of another example. This is the story of Manoj Vasaikar. He is an alumnus of my school. He found his uniqueness in food. So, he obtained a degree in catering management and got a job in London as a chef. He was trained in all the classical European cuisines by the best chefs in the best restaurants. He then had a different thought when he had the opportunity to start his own restaurant. He realized that he was an Indian chef in Europe, cooking European cuisine. He had no way to stand out. That is when he brought out his uniqueness as an Indian to start a restaurant called Indian Zing. He made it a Michelin-starred restaurant where he serves Maharashtrian food with a twist, paired with wines and other homemade drinks. He felt the joy in Indian cooking and leveraged it to make it one of the most popular restaurants in London.

Sometimes the answers may not come to you at once. In that case, start with something that really appeals to you. You will find the clues. You just need to keep looking for it. What you need to do is to embrace that you are different.

> *"Always be a first-rate version of yourself, instead of a second-rate version of somebody else."*
> – Judy Garland.

If you want to find your uniqueness in your professional life, you need to break it down into three periods. In the first ten years, look to acquire all the skills you need. In the next ten years, look to apply those acquired skills in contributing to all the stakeholders. Then in the next three years, establish your position.

This is when you create your own professional identity. You just have to live as yourself. When you work in the initial years, you need to be like a sponge and absorb all that you can from your peers. You need to be looking to upgrade your skills. When you embrace your quirks, you will be able to find opportunities to leverage them into your personal strengths.

It is vital that you never get into a 'Me-Too' mentality. When you get used to this approach, you become one of the masses. You will become just one who follows the group. You should never become a person who follows the group. You can be entrapped in a psychological phenomenon called Groupthink. It is a term first used by a social psychologist, Irving Janis, in 1972. Groupthink is a phenomenon where people try to find consensus. So, people will even set aside their own personal beliefs and values to find the group consensus. They will be intimidated to be the odd person out. Even if they are radically opposed to an idea, they will be timid. They will want to keep the peace instead of disrupting the group by standing up for their principles. You should know by now that there is one aspect of your life you should never compromise on—your values. Do not let the fear of rejection by others lead you to reject your ideas and convictions.

When you get entrapped by Groupthink, you will be paralyzed by self-censorship. You will constantly be weighing your words and how they would be received. You will never be honest. You will only be a safe and sanitized version of yourself, an illusion, who follows the crowd because of fear.

Even if you have some insight to share, you may keep quiet, thinking that the group knows best. If you notice, such thinking is repressive. You will slowly suffocate under the constant self-put-downs. You will start doubting yourself and your competency. Groupthink could also lead to risky behavior.

Look at any story of peer pressure gone wrong; you can trace it to Groupthink. Even when someone knows that a certain activity is wrong, they would still indulge in it because they would not want to disturb the harmony of the group.

Sometimes people also do not give a thought to the morality of their action as there would be others in the group who provide the validation for it. Groupthink has no place for an alternative opinion. It applies pressure on people to follow what it deems acceptable. You would lose your individuality in the process.

What is the consequence of losing your individuality? You lose the unique characteristics and thinking that made you, YOU. You will lose your creativity and would deprive the world of the wonders you could do. Think of any dystopian fiction. It can be classics like 1984, Brave New World.

Or it could be movies like Mad Max or Blade Runner. There is one common theme that unites them all. It is conforming to society. Do not conform. Confront the world; confront yourself. Then embrace yourself and then the world for all the diversity and variety it can provide.

"Here's to the crazy ones. The misfits. The rebels. The troublemakers. The round pegs in the square holes. The ones who see things differently. They're not fond of rules. And they have no respect for the status quo.
You can quote them, disagree with them, glorify or vilify them. But the only thing you can't do is ignore them because they change things!

They push the human race forward.
And while some may see them as the crazy ones, we see genius.
Because the people who are crazy enough to think they can change the world are
the ones who do!"
—Apple's Think Different marketing campaign in 1997

If you listen to the speech by Steve Jobs that preceded the Think Different marketing campaign, you can find many parallels to what I want to impress on you. He talks of how the world is noisy and how even Apple, as one of the best brands in the world, would not get a chance to remind people of their worth. He talks of how even a great brand needs investment and caring to retain its relevance and vitality. He then talks of the way one could do that. He stresses that it is not the technical stuff about the computers or how Apple is better than Windows. He references the Nike marketing campaign. Nike was a shoe company. But it never talked about its shoes in its advertisements. They honored great athletes and great athletics. They never talk of how they are better than their competitors. Those advertisements just conveyed what Nike was about.

Great athletes and great athletics! So, Steve Jobs borrowed a page from Nike's book with his 1997 Think Different campaign. He believed that there were people who wanted to change the world for the better, and Apple, too, wanted to change the world for the better. He talks of how the world and technology had changed. However, Apple, at its core, was about changing the world for the better. He remarks on how one's values and core values never change. So, Steve Jobs honored a lot of people in the advert. They all changed the world in their own way. He included people from Albert Einstein to Mahatma Gandhi, and Alfred Hitchcock to Muhammad Ali. Jobs would remark that some of these people would be living, and some of them would not be living and would never have used a computer. But then he cheekily adds that had they used a computer, it would have been a Mac. If there is one thing you should take from the advert, it is the line: ...*the people who are crazy enough to think they can change the world are the ones who do!*

One of the hidden traits needed for leadership is your individuality. You cannot lead when all you can do is follow. When you aspire for individuality, you will be inspiring. You will open avenues for creativity and innovation. When you discard the notions of what others think is acceptable, you will not be limited by ideas of what is possible and what is not possible.

You will tend to see the world in a different light. When the rest foresee a crisis, you will see opportunity. You can only be an effective leader when you are not scared of the doubts and fears of others. I am not suggesting that you become a dictator. You should be open to ideas and suggestions. However, you will not be limited by what other people think is impossible. When you lead from the front with such courage, your team members too will be encouraged to face their fears and conquer them.

The key thing to remember is that 'being you' has to become a daily habit. It cannot be switched on and off on a whim. Make a conscious decision to do something for yourself. It could be as simple as saying no to an activity you would rather not do.

Be confident and reclaim that space for yourself. Make increments in reclaiming your individuality. Even a small action like that will send a subconscious signal that you are prioritizing yourself over what others think is acceptable. Take time to reflect on your life. Use that time to reconnect with yourself. Think about your life, remind yourself about your goals, and check whether you are on track.

The mirror test is a great activity you can inculcate in your life. It can refocus your life. It will remind you of the important things in life. It will remind you of your values and show you where you strayed away from them. The mirror test can be the daily course correction you need as it makes you answer to your values and not to the values of others.

The one thing that we should never abandon is our inner child. As we grow older, we tend to discard it. We were the most expressive, honest, and curious when we were children. Reconnect with that inner child.

That honesty and curiosity will stand you in good stead. You need to be unafraid of who you are, just as you were in your childhood. During your time of reflection, you may also find that you have a lot of interests. You may feel overwhelmed by choice. Do not be burdened with the idea that you have to make the right choice. Trust your intuition and pick something and act on it. If you have been living based on the ideas of others and want to make a change, you may find saying no can be challenging.

As I mentioned before, start with some small activities that you do not want to continue doing. If you find that you cannot say no, write down a few alternative responses you could use. You could say something like, "I will have to think about it." If you feel that you have lost yourself in the process of fitting in, you have already made great progress. You have recognized the problem. Now you can work toward it.

"You are a marvel. You are unique. In all the years that have passed, there has never been another child like you. Your legs, your arms, your clever fingers, the way you move. You may become a Shakespeare, a Michelangelo, a Beethoven. You have the capacity for anything."
— Pablo Casal.

It was Winston Churchill who said that the kite rises against the wind and not with it. Dare to be different. When you wear the shoes fit for you by others, you will find your journey to be arduous and weary. You will limit your true potential and kill the fire and creativity that burn within you. So, aspire for the greatness that you are meant to achieve. Discard yourself of the toxic habits that make you look outward for approval. There is nothing wrong in wanting to feel wanted and included by others. But that is not a reason to discard your true self. Set your own dreams, and you will find that you have the capacity to chase them. I could have been easily discouraged from chasing my dream to be a CEO. I could have been discouraged by looking at my reality. I had no bankable last name, and I did not come from an affluent family with connections.

All I had was a dream, and I found the energy to make it come true. Be true to yourself, and you will be surprised to find the walls you shackled yourself in, crumble.

There is one final remark I want to make. Do not be different, just for the sake of it. There can be people who will be contrarian just because they want to be contrarian. Evaluate each situation on its merit and see where you stand. Then stand that ground. If you are not sure where you stand, you will know when you subject yourself to the mirror test.

Make it a habit to do it daily. When you remind yourself of your values daily, you will find that being yourself will not be as hard as you think.

"To be nobody but yourself in a world doing its best to make you everybody else means to fight the hardest battle any human can ever fight and never stop fighting."
— E. E. Cummings.

11

CREATE YOUR OWN PATH TO DESTINY

"No one saves us but ourselves. No one can, and no one may. we ourselves must walk the path."
— Buddha

We are governed by rules and laws. If we remember our childhood, we were warned not to play with fire or attempt to touch the flames. But we touched it nevertheless. A loud yelp and some singed skin with a burning sensation later, we knew why we were warned against it. Soon we came to know of different rules. We had to walk only on the footpath. The vehicles had to stick to one side of the road. We were then introduced to schooling, and we learned the rules of grammar for the languages we spoke. These rules were necessary. At some point in our life, we looked at everything through a black and white lens. There was a point when parents told their children that they could not become cricketers as there was no guaranteed income. Soon suggestions and sayings became rules which we could not cross. There is a reason why you were told these things. Parents did not want to douse the dreams of their young child wielding a wooden bat. They were just being pragmatic.

They did it with the best of intentions. However, we become boxed in by those suggestions. However, life is far more nuanced than following such a set pattern. There will be occasions where you question these rules. After all, these rules were set so that you could lead a happy life. But it is natural that at some point, you will feel unfulfilled. The rules have instead made you unhappy.

When you feel these emotions, take stock. Stop and take a step back. Reflect on the life you have lived and try to imagine the life you may lead henceforth. Does it particularly enthuse you? Are you traversing the path laid down by others? Maybe it is time you challenged those rules. It is your life, and there is nothing wrong in taking charge of it.

> *"Don't follow the path. Blaze the trail."*
> – Jordan Belfort

The first thing you should realize is that rules are never one-size-fits-all. The rules that worked for others may not work for you. Most people will tell you that a college education is a must for becoming successful. Look at some of the most successful entrepreneurs of today—Mark Zuckerberg, Richard Branson, and Bill Gates. They are all college dropouts. They blazed their own trails. They were not deterred by ideas of what was safe. They found a path they could walk upon, and they took it. All that you need is the desire.

One of the greatest stories in sports belongs to Nikki Lauda. Nikki, considered one of the greatest Formula 1 drivers, was at his prime form in 1976. The previous year, he had won the championship and was locked in a fascinating duel with his arch-rival and friend, James Hunt.

He was leading the championship once again. It was the German Grand Prix at the Nurburgring circuit. His car crashed and burst into flames. He inhaled toxic fumes that damaged his lungs and suffered from severe burns. He was presumed dead and was even given his last rites at the hospital. He had lapsed into a coma, but he survived. He had extensive scarring due to the burns.

He had lost most of his right ear and the hair on the right side of his head. He had also lost his eyebrows and eyelids. He opted for reconstructive surgery only for his eyelids. Six weeks after the accident, he was back on the track to defend his crown.

He had missed just two races, and in his first race back, he finished fourth. Nigel Roebuck, a journalist, would recall seeing Nikki in the pits, peeling off blood-soaked bandages from his scarred scalp. He had a specialized helmet to avoid discomfort.

He ran the championship close, losing to Hunt by only one point. Nikki returned the following year to win it again. He later remarked how terrified he was in his first race back, but he found his *joie de vivre* in the racing cockpit. So, he returned to it, contrary to all our assumptions that he probably would be afraid to do so.

I am not asking you to take a leap of faith without doing your research. If you feel the calling of a particular path, heed the call. However, do your research first. Speak to people and get their advice. Weigh the pros and cons. Once you are sure, take the leap. Trust your intuition.

"Have the courage to follow your heart and intuition. They somehow already know what you truly want to become. Everything else is secondary."
– Steve Jobs

One of the pitfalls you may stumble upon is the pressure you may heap on yourself. There is no hurry to make the 'right' decision. You cannot expect a red carpet to be laid out when you choose a path you want to pursue. There will be growing pains. It would be best to remember that there can be no failure to make a decision. It becomes a failure only when you refuse to learn and grow from your experiences. The mentality should always be about learning and not the ease of the path. Never be afraid of taking hold of an opportunity. Only be afraid if you keep your mind closed. A computer science graduate from Princeton got a lucrative career in Wall Street. He worked for firms like DE Shaw & Co., Fitel, and Bankers Trust.

However, at the age of 31, in late 1994, he was making a cross-country road trip from New York to Seattle.

He thought of an online bookstore and created a business plan during the trip. His name is Jeff Bezos, and he would evolve the online bookstore into one of the e-commerce giants, Amazon. Do not be overwhelmed by mistakes. No one is perfect. Whenever you start something new, it is natural to stumble. You are still learning the ins and outs of the situation. Embrace the opportunity. Failures will always reveal your hidden potential if you are looking to learn. Even if you do not attain the success you hoped for, learn the lessons and move forward.

When I got the opportunity in the 1990s to plant the flag for McCormick Spices in India, I learned from those hard knocks. I moved forward. I reminded myself that I wanted to be a CEO by the age of 45 and went to China. I want to stress that it is natural to be afraid when you look to carve your own path. You are abandoning the rules that were set for you to be safe. There is nothing wrong with being afraid.

The only mistake you can commit is if you refuse to face them. Confront your fears; no one expects you to be the most courageous person in the world. You just need the requisite amount of courage to face your fears. Everything new can seem scary and challenging. However, if you let your fears dictate your actions, you will never be able to live the life you want.

One of the fundamental life lessons you should engrave on your soul is to never give up. It may seem trite and cliched. However, remember nothing worthwhile is easy. It will demand your best and then ask you for some more. There will also be the temptation to give up at every slip and stumble. How will you respond? If I could tell you a story that would perfectly encapsulate the points that I have told you before, it would be the story of Billy Mills. In the 1964 Tokyo Olympics, after the 10,000-meter race, a Japanese reporter asked an American athlete a simple question, "Who are you?" Just a few minutes before that question was asked, this athlete had just won the 10,000-meter race.

The journalist's amazement and curiosity were natural as this athlete was an 'unknown' who had come out of nowhere to win the race. You see, the 26-year-old Billy Mills was no rising star. He had no achievements to his name, and he had qualified for the 1964 Olympics as a US Marine. It was a childhood dream of Mills to be an Olympic hero. He grew up an orphan, and he grew up in hard times. He was a half–Native-American, and he was forced to live with his tribe on a reservation. However, he had read an Olympic book as a child. It claimed that the Olympians were chosen by the Gods.

So, he wanted to be an Olympic champion as he thought it would lead him to heaven and he could meet his mother. He knew running would give him freedom. He broke the rules of what he could do as a Native American. He blazed his path and even won an athletic scholarship to go to the University of Kentucky.

But when he lined up in Tokyo for the 10,000-meter race, he was in the company of some celebrated athletes. There was Ron Clarke of Australia who held the world record. There was the defending champion, Pyotr Bolotnikov of the Soviet Union, and a New Zealander, Murray Halberg. During the heats, Mills' time was a minute slower than Clarke's time. This was not news to Mills. He used to keep a training journal. He had an excellent coach to help him train. However, he knew he was two minutes off the pace to win a gold medal. In a 10,000-meter race, reducing your best time by two minutes is akin to bridging an unbridgeable chasm.

Mills was not discouraged. He broke it down to putting a snap of energy per lap. In the final race, he kept close to Clarke throughout the race. On the last lap, he was boxed out and pushed by Clarke. He slipped, but he did not fall. He was now in third place. He would keep that pace until the final turn. Mills talks of how his mentality changed in the last section of the race. Even as he could only hear the throbbing of his heart, he kept saying to himself that he had won. His thoughts had changed from *'one more try; one more try'* to *'I can win, I can win.'* In one of the most iconic Olympic moments in history, Mills would barrel down the home stretch to win an Olympic Gold.

He was the first non-European to win the event and to this day is the only person to win Gold in this event from the North and South American continents.

"Do not follow where the path may lead. Go instead where there is no path and leave a trail."
– Ralph Waldo Emerson

There is one caution I would like to provide. When you want to carve your own path, do not carve the wrong one. History is rife with examples of people who went down the wrong path and lived to regret it. Modern India has one of the best examples you could find about dedication and commitment to your craft and values. Sachin Tendulkar and Vinod Kambli put on a world-record partnership as school children.

They had the perfect partnership. Tendulkar would be the calm, technical batsman to complement the dashing and attacking stroke player in Vinod Kambli. They were earmarked as future superstars of the game. They also shared the legendary coach, Ramakant Achrekar.

Kambli would have an explosive start as an international player. Within the first five innings of his international test career for India, he had scored back-to-back double hundreds and followed it up with two more centuries.

I am sure you have heard of the tale of Icarus, who flew too close to the sun. Kambli flew too close to the sun. His runs had dried up as he did not have the technique to ally his talent. He was known to enjoy his nights out as he indulged in the fame that came with the game.

Tendulkar, meanwhile, was disciplined. He worked hard, and after three years, he was already considered the mainstay of the Indian batting line-up. At the same time, Kambli was done as a test cricketer. Vinod Kambli would retire from the game by the age of 28. Sachin Tendulkar played for 11 more years, won the World Cup, and went down in history as one of the game's modern greats.

When the newspapers printed headlines about Tendulkar, it was about his match-winning feats, while in the case of Vinod Kambli, it was about his off-field issues. Then there is the case of Vijay Mallya. He inherited the breweries run by his father and converted it into one of the biggest beverage companies in the world.

To put it into context, when he inherited the company, they were selling about 2.5 million cases of spirits a year. Within 20 years, his company was selling 26 million cases. He introduced the idea of pub culture and masterminded some of the most creative surrogate advertisements to promote his products. He gave himself the moniker, The King of Good Times. He would also launch many ventures in sports. He became the owner of the IPL team, Royal Challengers Bangalore. He also acquired a Formula 1 team and named it Force India. He was also instrumental in putting India on the Formula 1 map with the Buddh International Circuit. He was a shrewd businessman.

However, today you will find him hiding in the UK to avoid the law in India. He failed in his airline venture and allegedly laundered money. His employees accused him of not paying their salaries. He was no longer the King of Good Times. I also remember a friend of mine. His name is Amir. He was my junior at school. If we ever had a survey of someone who would be the most successful, we would have all voted for Amir. He was extremely smart and hardworking. He always looked to improve himself. However, he lost his way at the age of 19. He found a way to make quick money. He would go to Dubai and buy items like gold chains etc., for lower prices and come back and sell it in India. He then increased the range of his operations.

One day he was caught, and his game was up. His quick money left him as quickly as he had obtained it. Today he is a man close to 50 years of age and has no house to his name. He takes part in many of our alumni activities. He gives talks to young and impressionable children about the dangers in the world. He warns them that they should not be seduced by such opportunities. So, it is imperative that you stay on the right path.

How will you know what the right path is? Subject yourself to the mirror test. If you feel guilty or embarrassed to share any activity of the day, you will know that you have strayed down the wrong path. I want to bring back and reinforce all the ideas that I wanted to share in this book. I want to remind you of a philosophy of mine: 'I can do it.' So, if you want to be successful in your life, here are some of the most important things you should possess:

1. **Ambition:**

   If you want to be successful, you first need a purpose. You can only draw a roadmap when you know where you want to go. You cannot just wish to be successful without purpose. If you do so, you are only enamored by the glamour and fame of success. You will never be able to put in the necessary work to achieve your goals.

   When you have no target to aim at, you will never be able to muster that extra 1% when you need it the most. I was driven by my ambition to be a CEO by the age of 45. I did not consider my limited background. I might have been from the chawl. But I wanted to be a CEO. That ambition dictated my actions for the rest of my life. I took up challenges that helped me grow until, finally, I realized my goal to be a CEO.

"It is a grand thing to rise in the world. The ambition to do so is the very salt of the earth. It is the parent of all enterprise, and the cause of all improvement."
   – Anthony Trollope

2. **Values:**

   If ambition provides you with the 'what' for your life, values give you the 'how' for it. They are the rules that you set for your life. If you fail those rules, no one is going to be more disappointed than you. Never compromise on your values. If you want to be truly successful, you cannot discount the importance of honesty and integrity.

When you fail your values to attain any success, that success will be tainted and transient. I can only stress the importance of the mirror test. This test has kept me on the straight and narrow. There was never a day when I was worried because I had to be honest when I stared into the mirror.

"Values are not just words; values are what we live by. They're about the causes that we champion and the people we fight for." – John F Kerry

3. **Adaptability:** No pursuit is going to be straightforward. You are bound to face many peaks and troughs in your quest for excellence. It will require you to be supple and flexible to handle these changes. When you are adaptable, you will not be pulled down by failure and equally not be swayed by your successes.

   To be adaptable, you have to keep an open mind. You have to be ready for change. It will help you to roll with the punches and keep you in the fight. It was when I went to China that I realized how important this life skill was. Keep an open mind because it will help you to handle all that life can throw at you. You only learn when you are receptive to it.

"Adaptability is not imitation. It means the power of resistance and assimilation." — Mahatma Gandhi.

4. **Perseverance:** When you chase something that you are interested in, there will come a time when you will want to give up. You will find that it is not as easy as you thought it was going to be. You may also be discouraged when you see someone else succeed. These are the moments when your commitment is tested. Once I had heard someone remark that perseverance begins when hard work has ended. Your tenacity is what keeps you on track when your mind may be screaming for you to stop.

5. **Humility:** Every success is a notch in your self-esteem. However, there is a danger of indulging in it for too long. It is humility that will also highlight your limitations. It will show you areas where you need improvement. Humility is what keeps you grounded. It helps to keep you on an even keel.

When you have humility, you will not be prideful in the face of praise or cowed down by failure. Humility helps in making you aware that there is a lot that you still need to learn. You will learn from the world and the different people you meet and interact with. If you are prideful, you will never find those opportunities.

"Humility is the proper estimate of oneself." – Charles Spurgeon.

Kobe Bryant would remark that when you have the mindset to become better, the world becomes your library. I have recounted my stories and the stories of other people because I want to impress upon you that there is no limit to your potential. Do not be limited by what you think you lack. Do not compare your circumstances to those of others. If you ever think you cannot do something, you will never do it.

If you want to achieve something, then think that you can do it. When you signal to yourself that you can do it, you will find the way to do it. Be hungry. Then think of how you will do it. Find your purpose and work toward it. It does not matter where you come from. It does not matter where you studied. It does not matter what you lack. What matters is your mindset. When you have a good mindset, you will enhance your skillset.

Even as you find your purpose, never forget your values. If there is one thing that I want you to take from my book, it is the mirror test. It is an exercise of accountability. It will keep you honest and make your life simpler. Even as the CEO of an MNC worth a million dollars, the mirror test helps me sleep peacefully. Think of any successful person; you will see that they have a rigid routine.

They have good habits. They have discipline and focus.

The mirror test is not just about your honesty. Are you trying to cultivate a good habit? The mirror test will help you stick to it.

So, as I leave you, I hope you find your purpose. I hope that you find the fire within you to pursue your goals. I learnt many lessons from many learned people across the world and was able to find my path and move forward. I have shared them with you in this book. Now you are all set with your wings outstretched. Fly high into the skies and blaze a trail for yourself.

"Without ambition one starts at nothing. Without work one finishes nothing. The prize will not be sent to you. You have to win it."
— Ralph Waldo Emerson

ABOUT THE AUTHOR

From Management Trainee to Chairman & Managing Director

Satish Rao is a veteran in corporate circles and is presently serving as the Chairman & Managing Director at Firmenich India Aromatics Ltd. Firmenich is a Swiss multinational company and the world's largest privately held Fragrance & Taste company. Satish has 30 years of experience spread across the Chemicals and Food industry and has worked in key economies of the world like China, the USA, and India.

Satish has been very active in social community welfare initiatives, exemplified by his role as the Founder President of his school's alumni association in Mumbai and the Indian Association in China. He is passionate about sharing his learnings from across the three continents that he has worked in, and has done so in this book through real-life examples. He wants to let people know that one's background means nothing in the pursuit of success, and through this book, he distills some practical life tips on how to articulate life mission and how you can accomplish it.